DATE DUE OCT 0 6

GAYLORD			PRINTED IN U.S.A.

DESTINED FOR DESTINY

The Unauthorized Autobiography of George W. Bush

SCRIBNER

NEW YORK   LONDON   TORONTO   SYDNEY

JACKSON COUNTY LIBRARY SERVICES
MEDFORD OREGON 97501

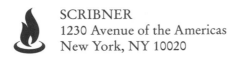

SCRIBNER
1230 Avenue of the Americas
New York, NY 10020

This book is a work of fiction. Names, characters, places, and
incidents either are products of the authors' imagination or are used
fictitiously. Any resemblance to actual events or locales or persons,
living or dead, is entirely satirical.

Copyright ©2006 by DH News Service, LLC
All rights reserved, including the right of reproduction in whole or
in part in any form.

SCRIBNER and design are trademarks of Macmillan Library
Reference USA, Inc. used under license by Simon & Schuster, the
publisher of this work.

Designed by Rick Martin
Set in Stempel Garamond

Manufactured in the United States of America

10 9 8 7 6 5 4 3 2 1

Library of Congress Cataloging-in-Publication Data

ISBN-13: 978-0-7432-9966-4
ISBN-10:   0-7432-9966-3

For information regarding special discounts for bulk purchases,
please contact Simon & Schuster Special Sales at 1-800-456-6798 or
business@simonandschuster.com.

For the faith-havers

CONTENTS

ACKNOWLEDGMENTS

Two fine authors made this important book come to life: Peter Hilleren and Scott Dikkers. These were the right men at the right time in a crucial moment in our nation's history—a time when a book about me needed to be written.

I thank Susan Moldow, Nan Graham, Beth Wareham, and all the good folks at Scribner for their unwavering support of the *Destined for Destiny* plan for victory. Special thanks is due to editor Brant Rumble for his honorable service to my vision, and his wisdom of the bookmaking craft.

Agent Jonathon Lazear deserves my praise for his steadfast search for the right home for this manuscript, his tireless moral support, and his loyalty to the Bush family. Thanks also to Dan Greenberg for his gracious help in the early stages of this work.

The combined guidance and expertise of John Fulbrook, Colin Tierney, Marcellus Hall, Mike Loew, and especially Rick Martin were indispensable in culling the archival documents, newspaper clippings, and other images from my life. They did the hard work and the research that I would not. I am also grateful to Colin Strohm for his unparalleled skill in restoring historical photographs. And Brandt Wagner is forever accepted into my heart for his divine grace and superb modeling ability.

Proofreaders Andy Goldwasser, Laura Wise, and Margaret Meehan have earned my respect for their eagle-eyed attention to detail, which surpassed even that of the sages.

Thanks to all the good people at *The Onion* who offered their strong support and understanding during the writing of this book. I do not read *The Onion*, but I understand it is one of our nation's leading newspapers.

I also would like to express our sincere gratitude to my family and friends for patiently enduring the few occasions when the writing of this book intruded on their otherwise happy lives.

Most importantly, I wish to thank myself. I provided these gifted typers with a rich and never-ending well of material that is certain to leave its indelible mark on not only their lives, but on the lives of everyone on the planet Earth, for generations to come.

George W. Bush
Crawford, TX
July 24, 2006

INTRODUCTION

By Vice President Dick Cheney

I'd like to begin my introductory remarks by stating unequivocally that the Bush Administration has not authorized this work.

I advised the President that this was not the appropriate time to release a book containing highly classified information which may compromise our nation's security. I warned that the release of a work so revealing could result in another terrorist attack on our country, one that would be many thousands of times worse than 9-11.

This was my view based on the evidence, and had nothing to do with the fact that the President had still not given me an autographed copy of the book, for which my feelings were deeply hurt.

Nonetheless, the President announced that he had made his decision—a firm decision—to publish this book, and that was the end of it. I stand by his leadership, regardless of how many innocent people must die.

It has been my great privilege to serve alongside a leader of the caliber of George W. Bush, without question the finest President who has ever occupied the White House. His fortitude in the face of evil has been, frankly, kick-ass.

I enjoy a certain amount of objectivity with regard to the President's record of achievement. The reason being that I have no political ambitions beyond my current duties as Vice President. The fact is, I have no ambitions beyond completing the dictating of this sentence without suffering a fatal coronary embolism.

Most days I sit in the shadows of my hygienically sealed, temperature-controlled command center, clinging tenuously to life, my tiny black heart squeezing out a cold trickle of blood to my cerebral cortex with every strained and painful pump. I sit stoop-backed over a bank of computers and phones connecting me to every U.S. agency so that I may conduct the affairs of state from this secret location, which is inaccessible except by military pass through several feet of solid lead and tachyon shielding beneath a remote airbase that does not appear on any world map.

I emerge only for the occasional speech to the Competitive Enterprise Institute, luncheons with the Petroleum CEOs of America, and invigorating hunting trips where my ambulance drives me directly in front of a cowering, helpless bird, which I then shoot in the face at point-blank range.

I also come out every Saturday morning for my weekend workshops on interpretive dance for underprivileged kids in East St. Louis. I really enjoy working with those kids.

I'd like to reflect, if I might, on the first time I met George W. Bush as a young man. In his father's White House he was the sharp understudy who showed great curiosity for carrying out the perfect practical joke on old man Cheney. I didn't particularly appreciate it, but I witnessed a certain bold resolve, a talent for innovative thinking, when he lodged a pork wiener in the fly of my slacks so that it flopped straight out just as I stood to greet the Chinese Premier at an important state dinner.

And I shared in his delight, retrospectively, for the many times he placed a tack on my office chair. He displayed a tremendous amount of joy and zest for life when I jumped out of my seat, clutching my behind and howling like a wounded animal. There was also the exploding of the beer keg in the East Room, and the numerous circumstances in which he displayed his formidable instincts with a whoopee cushion, most notably as it related to senior administration officials during high-level cabinet meetings.

Suffice it to say, I knew this was a future world leader of extraordinary promise.

When then-Governor Bush handpicked me to screen myself for the position of vice-presidential candidate in 2000, I felt what I believed at the time to be a genuine surge of excitement. Either that or I had suffered a major pacemaker malfunction.

Before recommending myself for the role of the Vice Presidential candidate, I looked at myself very carefully, asking all the tough questions. I recall that I fared pretty well under my scrutiny. I gave me a tough but fair hearing. How's my heart, I asked. Do I think I can stand the stress? Yes, I believe I can, I answered. Will you serve the President, loyally, faithfully, honorably? Absolutely. My loyalties are clear, I said confidently. The office would come second only to my service to Christ and the Halliburton board of directors.

The day I received the phone call from myself announcing that I had accepted the job was the happiest of my life. I felt a faith in humanity—a feeling of warmth I hadn't experienced since the days of the Vietnam War, when I bonded with my fellow men, men who also had other priorities besides fighting.

Throughout the years, I have been impressed with George W. Bush's quick wit and keen intellect. When we first met, he smirked broadly while we were shaking hands, then made up an enduring nickname for me right on the spot. Quasimodo. For the last 30 to 35 years that's what the entire Bush family has called me. Frankly, I'm a bit tired of it.

But this is neither the time nor the place to air such grievances. This is the time to express my deep and lasting respect for George W. Bush, a Commander in Chief of exceptional capabilities, and to extol this great autobiographic work, which is destined to become a classic of political writing—a "must read," if you will.

One thing is clear. I am confident that the President's beautifully written tales of heroism and triumph over adversity herein will inspire, in significant measure, laughter, thrills, and even weeping in a vast majority of readers.

Candidly, I found myself moved to tears by these inspiring accounts of a great man's life and leadership. Rather, I would have been, had my tear ducts not been stapled shut as part of a radial keratectomy procedure I underwent in 1994 for an advanced case of degenerative myopia.

Now I must conclude my remarks, and turn my attentions back to my official responsibilities here in the underground bunker, where, hunched over my high-tech control console, I am working diligently to perpetuate the permanent state of war and unlimited, almost monarchical rule that our Founding Fathers envisioned, stopping only occasionally to cough up some liver bile and open a shareholder letter informing me of my cut of another quarter's record Halliburton profits, with which I intend to purchase nothing but precious, life-giving saltines, the only form of sustenance my brittle and cancerous insides can digest.

Now, please go fuck yourself.

DESTINED FOR DESTINY

1

LIKE "ROOTS" ONLY WHITE

In the great American TV program "Roots," author Kunta Kinte traced his ancestry back to the early times in our history.

My heart was touched by this great drama of history. That is why I intend to embark upon the same journey in this chapter. It may not be as interesting as "Roots," since it will not be filled with the rich tapestry of culture enjoyed by our blacks, and it will not feature all of the wonderfully colorful slave names which are so entertaining to listen to when the old-time blacks say them with their funny accents. But it will reveal the history of the Bush family, from the pre-historical times of my grandfather all the way to the present times.

To understand a leader, one need not necessarily look into the past to that particular leader's noble forebears to gain insight into that leader's qualities and the "stuff" that he is made of. History has no bearing on the present. One must only look at the kind of man he has grown up to be. Is he likened to the great oak, which will not waiver in the face of the winds of the opposers? Or is he like the mighty rock, which steadfastly governs his fellow man with immobile resolve and the wisdom of the stones?

In this first chapter of my autobiography, we will take a momentous ancestral journey through my life in which new facts may come to light, creating a context to understand the man who leads our nation.

But let there be no misunderstanding. I will not do any research for this book. That is not the kind of journey I am talking about. I believe that if a book is to be an accurate account of a man's life and times, it must come from the heart, and not from dusty old volumes with a lot of complicated words and pages yellowed by the eons.

What I know is this: In the beginning, the universe was a formless void. Then on the first day, God created Adam. Next there were a series of generations that came and went upon the Earth. Finally, some 100 years ago, my grandfather, Prescott Bush was born.

Prescott Bush served with distinction as a United States Senator, I am told. His son, George H. W. Bush, also heeded the call of public service and was elected President in the last century, serving one term in which a Great War was begun with a bold code name and determined theme music.

In contrast, I am now a two-term President. Will there be a third? It is a hypotheoretical question to which only the prophets can know the answer.

It is worth noting that each new generation of the Bush family achieves more accomplishments than the last.

Who knows where it all will lead? Will my brother Jeb follow my success with an accomplished administration of his own? Will my daughters serve as twin Presidents who will reign for eight years after that? Or perhaps, one of my daughters will be President, and the other will be Vice President, and then the Vice President will become the President, and vice versa, so that there will be a Bush in the White House for seven generations. Would the constitutional lawyers allow such a scenario? No one can say. The sheer number of possibilities are enough to confuse the mind.

One thing is clear. There will always be members of the Bush family ready to answer the call to serve their country and steer it off the cliff of greatness.

But that is not what this first chapter is about. This is not a chapter about future-times. It is one about the times of history. The history of the Bush name.

As I have said, Prescott Bush lived in an ancient and simpler time, a time when we were not fighting a global war against the enemies of freedom like today. It was a long-ago time of peace and tranquility, the 1930s and 40s.

My grandfather demonstrated my family's high ideals and business sense in the area of entrepreneuring. He was a successful banker and merchant who made his fortune by wisely investing in a promising foreign country. It was a country whose fortunes were changing for the better, and who had a promising future under the steady hand of an inspirational leader.

The proud troops of this country marched through the streets of the cities in gleaming uniforms and shiny

The view from our back hut window was unacceptable, and become tolerable only when we woke some of the locals and insisted that we be moved to more tasteful quarters.

December the Twelfth — The beastly Connecticutt winter has been ladened with difficulties most enormous. The servants, including six of our best negroes, may not last the month. The servants have entreated me to equip their quarters with a wood-burning stove for heating, but such would violate Christian principles. The Lord has deprived them of wealth, therefore hath forsaken them. I shall not question the wisdom of the Almighty.

January the Twenty Eighth — A perilous journey indeed from the wilderness to the port of New Amsterdam, to rendezvous with our banker on Wall Street. Desperate cold I imagine, for our horses, though we could not see them from inside our carriage. The wheels kicked up snow that sometimes could be seen from our window. My dear Hermina clutched her mink shawl close to her bosom to stave off a violent case of the discomforts.

March the Tenth — During another grueling days travel, my top hat nearly fell off my head and onto the fox-skinned rug at my feet. Promptly served the driver with fifty lashes.

Journal page from unknown Bush ancestor, circa 1800

black boots that would goose-step high and proud. The great leader was hailed by his people with outstretched arms of awe and wonder.

It took a savvy investor like my grandfather to see that this was an excellent business opportunity—a country that was going places. An industrious nation that operated with military-like precision, tolerating nothing but pure perfection in all of its undertakings and citizenry.

This strong and patriotic country grew to become one of the leading economic and political powers in all of Europe, eventually surpassing all the world in its manufacture of fine automobiles and electric shavers.

Prescott Bush also was a devoted family man, passing along his talent for business and politics on to his eldest son, George H. W. Bush, who would become my father.

My father met my mother at a debutante party when she was 30. He was immediately enchanted by her horselike beauty, her forceful nature, and her immense stature. She loved his gangly limbs, and his rugged, upper-crust Connecticut standing.

Barbara Bush, who my mother is also known as, was a good-hearted and strict woman, descended from hardy stock. She was sired and fed to an impressive girth by a wealthy family, led by her father, whose hard work had built a fortune in the doily business.

Life was not easy in Doily Country. Many families worked all day to create the fine doilies, often suffering from frillyitis of the forearms and fingers. This of course is caused by the repetitious and exacting movements required to manipulate the tiny threads into one-of-a-kind doily patterns.

My mother narrowly escaped this fate, as her stumplike fingers were unsuited for doily weaving. She found a place in the family business, not as a mill worker, sewing the lacy, ornamental napkins and coasters, but in the parlors of customers, placing the doilies on armchairs and Victorian fainting couches throughout the land.

It was a hard life, but a dainty one. My mother would survive the great trial of her doily-placing toil, inherit a great doily legacy, and live her life surrounded by doilies. She would be consumed by the lacy ornaments, wearing them around her neck and her face. During lean times, she would be forced to boil doily remnants in water to make doily soup, or put them on stale bread with doilyonnaise to make sandwiches to feed her children.

My mother wears doilies to this day, and insists they cover every surface she touches. The doily is the proud symbol of her family's history.

Yet it conflicted with her inner nature, her true heritage of eons past.

Family legend tells that Barbara Bush's genealogy goes back to the Visigoth hordes, a strong and unwavering clan of warriors who laid siege to the Lands of the Ancient Kings. With their battle-axes and lances, they would leave nothing but ruin and blood in their wake, taking donkeys as their brides.

Apart from my mother, my father, George H. W. Bush, is the finest man I ever knew. He was born in a mud hut, in Kennebunkport, Maine. His father, the modest state senator and landowner of whom I have already written a great deal (see preceding pages), taught him the value of hard work.

My father hauled bank notes and securities by hand through the New England snow, carrying buckets of money from his father's banks all the way to the family's makeshift estate in the Kennebunkport, Maine territory. His spirits refused to be daunted by the hard work, and as the sun set, you could often hear his lyrical and beautiful money-hauling song float across the countryside.

My father's humble beginnings would eventually lead him to the highest office in the land. But to get there, he would have to make the ultimate sacrifice, and give his life during the Great War.

It was a sad loss for our family, but a proud loss, for he had died fighting for America's freedom against the feared Burmese.

After the war, his death would be commemorated by a grateful nation, who proudly elected him to the House of Representatives in Texas—the first corpse to ever attain such a high honor. He served with distinction, fighting for the rights of all undead Texans during the turbulent Civil Rights era of the 1950s and 60s.

He would be offered the Chairmanship of the Republican Party, the first-ever Zombie to hold that post, and a singular honor for a dead man in the years of the Nixon administration. He was the standard bearer of Republican virtue during this time, and looked on proudly with his dead, black eyes.

My father would hold many important posts in public life in the coming years, and in some, I would play modest parts.

We will get to such achievements in due time, but for now, we move to the next phase of my life, the part where it begins.

2

A LEGACY OF DESTINY

I am not one to obsess over the details of history. But I can report with a great deal of certainty that I was born at some time in July, 1946.

However, I believe in a culture of life. Therefore it is my view that I was born long before I was born. The date I began life as an unborn warrants equal recognition as a momentous date in history. Some laws would have you believe I was not a full citizen until I was born the second time. But I believe that God's law supercedes man's law. And God's law states that life begins when I say.

Having said that, I believe it is inappropriate to investigate the date of my conception. It would be an overly burdensome and delicate undertaking involving complicated calculations and tough questions.

In the years in which I was born, it was the golden time of America's peacetime after a Great War. A World War that spawned a Great Generation, many of whom paid the ultimate sacrifice, and won a great victory over tyranny, defeating the hated invaders, the China-men.

My father and mother had played their part in that generation. Therefore I was a child of war.

Some have said that at the time of my birth a great star shone in the night sky, shining brighter than the rest, and it marked my birth in the Heavens. Stars can do that, which verifies what scientists teach us regarding the nature of stars.

A poor man and his wife traveling in Kennebunkport, Maine could not find room in the inn. So it was there that George H. W. Bush and his wife, Barbara, who was great with child, lay down in a straw barn, not knowing the great portents of these happenings.

Legend also says that in attendance at my birth were three wise Republican political consultants, who followed the birth-marking star, traveling a great distance to the parents of the newborn babe to bestow upon me great gifts of jewels, frankincense, and a campaign contribution for my father's upcoming congressional race. It was a true miracle.

A great and powerful Angel appeared to Barbara and George that night, saying, "Lo, your son born unto the world this night will grow up to be a great leader, a leader who will lead a people to freedom from a brutal dictator not yet born."

These Angel's words have unquestionably come to pass, and it is my view that this story is an accurate account. Some have said there were no wise men present at

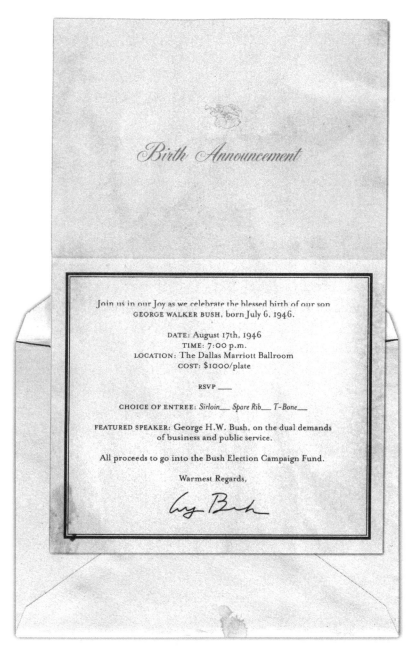

Join us in our Joy as we celebrate the blessed birth of our son
GEORGE WALKER BUSH, born July 6, 1946.

DATE: August 17th, 1946
TIME: 7:00 p.m.
LOCATION: The Dallas Marriott Ballroom
COST: $1000/plate

RSVP ___

CHOICE OF ENTREE: *Sirloin*___ *Spare Rib*___ *T-Bone*___

FEATURED SPEAKER: George H.W. Bush, on the dual demands
of business and public service.

All proceeds to go into the Bush Election Campaign Fund.

Warmest Regards,

Birth announcement card, August, 1946

my birth, according to the hospital records that have been released. However, it has been confirmed that one of the nurses had at one time been a shepherd.

It is an interesting fact that the Angel had been aware not only of my birth but the birth of the brutal dictator I would one day face. He had the power to foretell the full details of the prophecy concerning me, the war, and all the related events—a complicated process, even for a great and wise Angel.

It electrifies the mind to contemplate the intricate workings of the Lord of Hosts, who must have offered aid to this Heavenly Agent, and worked in concert with the dark forces, perhaps allowing Satan to mate with a human female to create this future opponent for me. The otherworldly machinations of these mysteries cannot be known to mortal men.

Regardlessness, from the earliest moments it was clear that I was a child of destiny. What would that destiny be? Only the storied fates would know.

I believe it was the wise Billy Graham, who would later play a pivotal role in my spiritual life, who first noted the signs of my coming role in future times. It is said that he pointed out to my mother, "Behold, a child of great promise."

He revealed to my mother the evidence at hand: that I ate off only the finest china, that I suckled from bottles made of the finest blown glass, and drank only the finest, richest milk. My blankets were always fresh and clean—and swaddling—and were made of the finest silk and flamingo-down stuffing, which had to be washed by hand, gently. I myself was bathed by attendants and anointed with sweet-lotions and powders.

Surely these were the trappings of a future leader of men, a great tool of the Lord.

But it would not all go so smoothly on a path from promising infant to War President of prophecy.

Soon after I was born, my mother and father placed their swaddling infant in swaddling clothes, and I proceeded to swaddle. In fact, I swaddled uncontrollably for seven days and nights.

They began to grow concerned.

They tried covering me in more swaddling clothes and tightly swaddled blankets and even a magnificent swaddling cape. But nothing would stem the swaddle. Swaddling does not normally go on for so long, especially with such high-quality infant-wear.

They called for a doctor, a swaddlhiatry specialist. He applied a swadpository ointment. But it was to no avail.

My mother and father were preparing for the worst, loading up the car for a long stay at the hospital. In those days, an infant had a recovery period of two to three weeks following a swaddlectomy. Thankfully the swaddling went into remission, and I emerged, a young baby full of promise and hope.

From that moment, my mother and father knew there was something different about me. They would feed me baby food and I would dribble it all over my lip, turning mealtime into chaos. They would attempt to feed me Cheerios, and I would smash them with my tiny fists on my high-chair tray. When it came time for bed, often I would not sleep through the whole night. I would sometimes awaken at odd hours, and cry and cry.

Clearly at every turn, I was an extraordinary child. I was a fighter.

Perhaps it was clear at that point, looking back at it, that I would grow to be a War President. A President who would never shrink from a fight, who would take on the greatest challenges of the 21st century, such as the defeat of evil.

Like peas in a bowl, I would go on to smash the dictators with a spoon. I would squish the terrorists in my hands like a warm pork wiener, and watch them ooze out between my clenched fingers. I would squash the enemies of freedom like macaroni and cheese until they were nothing but a yellow pulp on my plate. I would smear the evil dictators all over my bib.

When I was a toddler, the high chair was my throne, a great perch from which I would decide which foods were to be my favorites. Wieners made the cut. Green beans did not.

I grabbed handfuls of beans and hurled them out of sight the best I could. Our dog, Buster, gobbled them up as soon as they landed on the floor. But my mother glared at me, trying to will me into eating those beans.

But I did not yield. It was then, when faced with a fierce opponent, that I learned the importance of standing one's ground. I would remain at the dinner table as long as it took to finish the job. I would feed that dog all of my beans.

My mother was a critic of this eating strategy. As with all critics, I did not spend time puzzling over her words. I pursued a strategy that was working. And hurtling beans on the floor for the dog to eat was working. I had the facts to back up my strategy. Buster liked the beans. And there were none left by the time I was through eating. No one can refute these successes.

This tactic was vital to mealtime. If I had stopped feeding beans to the dog, it would have dishonored all the beans I had already thrown. To honor the sacrifice of these fallen beans, I had to continue to throw beans to the dog.

Deep down I knew that my mother was a worthy opponent. For reasons unknown, she refused to suckle me, and therefore my sustenance came from the baby bottle. I do not fully understand why my mother used this method. And I do not reflect on such things at this late stage in life.

But I do know that the bottle became my friend. I was always reaching for it, and felt empty without its sweet nectar at my lips. I believe I was four years old before I gave it up. My mother wrested it from my tightly gripped little hands over my wailing protestations. No matter how loudly I demanded it, she would not give it to me.

During those dark times, my father would read me a bedtime story. Usually it involved a heroic U.S. Senator finding oil in Texas. Sometimes the Senator would get a historic bill passed. It was hard for me to get to sleep afterwards, with stories so thrilling.

He also told me stories of far-off sandy lands of great wealth and opulence, filled with more oil than a nation could possibly use in a century. His eyes would mist over as he spoke of the Arab princes with their hundred wives and a hundred more oil wells. He said, "Son, remember, having a hundred wives is wrong."

To this day that adage has guided me.

3

NO BUSH CHILD
LEFT BEHIND

There is something that I must confess about my childhood. It was, at times, a difficult struggle.

I realize that a President is expected to recollect fondly on his childhood years, with golden sunsets on a family farm, drinking milk, doing chores, and learning the value of a dollar.

But my early years were a tough road of hardships.

My parents were simple oil folks. My father barely made enough money in the family oil farm to keep my mother in pearls. He worked long, hard hours, was rarely in the home, and when he ventured out on his own, in the uncertain Texas oil business, we all had to pull extra weight.

I remember grueling chores, in which I had to haul buckets of oil money from the car to the house. And there was a great deal of discipline when chores were not completed satisfactorily.

To enforce this discipline, my mother used what we called the "spanking board."

It was a bread-cutting board with a handle, made out of thick oak hardwood. Perhaps in a long-ago time it was smooth, but after years of slicing cucumber sandwiches, it had gained a rough and splintery surface.

I accepted this as a show of love and respect. Tough love. You cannot have toughness without love, nor loveness without tough.

One particularly defining tragedy that occurred in my life took place when I was six. I fell and skinned my knee.

My mother comforted me as best she could. Never one to touch a child directly, she quickly summoned a nanny. That nanny bundled me up in warm blankets, and suckled the gravel from my torn flesh. She dabbed tentatively at my tear-stained cheeks with a laced handkerchief. She gave me warm milk and buttered cakes, until my little belly was round and full. She tucked me in my warm, soft bed and comforted me as I cried and cried from the pain.

Later, I would learn that my father had come home after I had fallen asleep and asked his secretary to write me a check for $1,000 to further ease my intense discomfort.

That night, visions of painful asphalt filled my nightmares. It was a hellish night I would never forget. But the important thing is that I had faced my fears. The horror of this incident did not defeat me. It made me stronger.

To this day, I still draw upon that torturous memory for strength in difficult times.

One aspect of my childhood that I recall with some fondness is my warm friendship with Mr. Bigsby, my

FROM THE DESK OF
GEORGE. H. W. BUSH

Dear Son,

It was with great pleasure to bounce you on my knee
last night. I sincerely hope we have the opportunity
to do the same again soon.

Warmest Personal Regards,

George. H. W. Bush

First note received from father, October 22, 1947

best friend. He was an invisible boy who played with me whenever I wanted to play.

Mr. Bigsby helped me see the brighter side.

He helped me see that my childhood was not all tragedy. My toys, for example, brought me much joy. I derived great pleasure from taking my battleships and tanks and little plastic men out into the back yard to create a play-battle, one that typically ended with them getting blown up somehow, or mashed beneath my feet in a terrible imaginary struggle in which many toy soldiers melted, broke, or were tragically lost, battling the feet of a mighty goliath.

Let us take a moment of silence to remember those toy soldiers.

Every President has one moment in his childhood that he credits with being the formative experience of his life. One of the earliest Presidents of America, George Washington, went to his father and admitted that he had chopped down the cherry tree, saying, "I cannot tell a lie." Abraham Lincoln wrestled a Kentucky log cabin to the ground. And Ronald Reagan vanquished Pancho Villa to found the new territory of California.

I had a similar defining moment.

Mr. Bigsby came to me one day and said, "Hey, let's go torture some frogs." And I said, "Sounds like fun."

After that, I could not get enough of the joyous wonder that is frog torture. Frogs were truly a gift of God's creation. Bouncing playthings one could collect and torment endlessly without it ever becoming boring.

I had collected a few frogs one summer's eve, and was prepared to toss them all in a big clump against the wall of our garage, where they would burst in one glorious bloody sploosh. Just as my arm was cocked back, however, my father came up behind me and said, "George, what are you doing?"

I told him I was going to watch these frogs splat against the wall.

He looked at me for a moment with his sad eyes and said, "Be sure to get one of the servants to help you clean that up when you are done."

It was an important lesson in delegating responsibility that I would never forget. One cannot discount the influence a father has on the developing scruples of a young boy. Time and again, my father's influence during my youth would mold me into the man I am today.

But more important than a parent are the choices one makes which form a President's morals. These are the great trials in life in which one learns the importance of personal responsibility for one's actions. This is especially important in a President, who must lead a people.

I recall the precise moment in my life when my ethical compass was forged.

It was a bright summer day in Texas. While playing in the garage, I encountered a box of firecrackers. It was a spectacular, bright yellow package, and the firecrackers were the kind with the little cylinders and the little fuse like miniature sticks of dynamite, and they were in a pristine, sealed box, waiting to be torn open. One could even smell the intoxicating fumes of the gunpowder within.

I was faced with an ethical dilemma which would define my moral principles for years to come.

I could, as I saw it, do one of two things.

One, I could light the firecrackers in the back yard.

Two, I could take them to the quarry where I had much less chance of being caught, and stuff them up the buttholes of frogs that I had collected, then watch them explode, with guts and frog legs flying in every direction, and thereby enjoy a good laugh.

It is perhaps obvious which path I chose to follow.

4

TEACHER'S PEST

As I entered my school years, I began to realize the burden that was upon me to excel. I looked at the long line of Bush ancestors whose pictures hung on our living-room wall, and I realized that these pictures of my family were destined for something special. They were destined to lead.

I thought of the strange two-dimensional world these forebearing ancestrals had to live in. A world of black and white, where they were surrounded on all sides by fine wooden picture frames. Yet they thrived and became the masters of their times.

Therefore, as a Bush, I was held to a higher standard in education, not bound by the same rules as others.

I am not talking about a kind of special pass that comes

from the idea that "my dad is a powerful oil executive so I should get special privileges." That would be unfair and unjust in our country. I am talking about a kind of special pass that comes from God.

But I quickly learned that you cannot always get special treatment in life.

Some days in school I sat next to children who were from the cattle ranches, and no matter how hard they may have tried, they could not get the stink of the cattle farm off of themselves. The tolerance I learned while sitting next to these other children, being exposed to their strong smell, has served me well as President. I will speak in more detail about this in a later chapter, the chapter about the human sense of smell, in which I detail the mechanism that nose glands use to detect odors.

My true personality came out during those early years of my education. Teachers and students alike quickly learned that I was the kind of child that you could sit down and have a chocolate milk with. I made friends easily, and those I could not make friends with, I would tease relentlessly until I was assured of their loyalty.

I met a boy in elementary school who was to become a life-long friend. Albert Tolliver. I tormented him endlessly with taunts, teasing, and bullying. Yet he always came back to me and said, "George, you are my best friend." Once his loyalty was proven to me, which took many cruel and dangerous tests, I allowed him to become a dear friend. We have remained close to this day. His wife and two lovely children have joined Laura and me for dinner on many occasions.

Before his wife and children first came over, however, I had to subject them to the same battery of grueling loy-

Ector County Public Schools
Report Card

Report of *George Bush*

Age *8*   Grade *2*   Dist. No. *19*

Teacher *Mrs Weiner*

	1st Qtr	2nd Qtr	3rd Qtr	4th Qtr
Arithmetic	C+	B	A-	A
Reading	D+	A-	A	A
Writing	C+	C+	B+	B+
Spelling	B-	C+	B	D+
U.S. History	C	D	A	A+
Civics	C+	C	D	A+
Phys-Ed	B	B-	B	B+

Parents Signature *Barbara Bush*   Date *May 26 '54*

Third-grade report card from Midland Elementary School

alty tests. They were each taped to the flagpole, forced to put their tongues on a freezing cold monkey bar in the dead of winter, and repeatedly dunked head first into the toilet bowl. But after these preliminary trials, we proceeded to have a pleasant meal.

I would make up friendly nicknames for the other kids, such as Spanky, Nosy, Big Lips, and Flat Head. Even the teachers could not escape my wanton nicknaming. When I made a nickname, it stuck. One of my teachers was named "Mr. Whiston." I gave him the name of "Mr. Dizzy Whizzy," because he was a science teacher who had outlandish theories like, for example, the one about the earth orbiting the sun, which flew in the face of common sense.

And there was Mrs. Beasley, who I called "Mrs. Beeswax" because she was always in other people's beeswax, or "business," as the grammarians call it now. Every time I turned around she was there, buzzing around, keeping her vulture's eyes on me. I stayed after school on more than one occasion because of her beeswaxiness.

I was what educators call a "hands on" learner, in other words, someone who does not learn best from lessons in school, but lessons in life. It is how I learned to talk. It is how I learned to walk. And it is how I learned to govern.

There is only so much you can go learn from books. When you are learning with a book, many times you have to set the book aside, roll up your sleeves, and take action, possibly getting your hands dirty and doing a lot of damage to the book.

School is for all types of learners, however. It is up to the teachers to separate the wheat from the chaff. They need to take the time to know each of their students in the classroom, then tailor a learning program particularly for each student, then round up all the ones who do not make the grade, and expel them.

When I enrolled in elementary school, I went in with a solid grounding in key subjects. My mother and father, as well as my own horse sense, had prepared me well regarding the basic facts of math, science, and reading.

So when my new teacher, Mrs. Fatty, tried to instruct me in these subjects, I knew right away that we would have a difference of opinion on the facts. In the matter of multiplication tables, for example, she insisted on teaching me and the other students that 3 times 2 equaled 6. But I felt strongly that it equaled 9. This was one of those tired ideas put forth by the intellectuals, and it had little or no bearing on how things panned out in the real world.

I knew it was 9 because I believed it was 9, and this was a cherished belief handed down for generations in my family. Rest assured, it would take a lot more than a bunch of dusty old mathematics texts to shake my faith in this fact.

In the face of this impasse of educational philosophies, I relied on the sound judgment of my dad and his powerful influence in Texas schools at that time. The outcome of this particular classroom disagreement was fair and equitable for both me and the teacher.

Let me put it this way: In short order, that particular teacher was no longer teaching her brand of outmoded math.

But let us start at the beginning. My first day of school was a traumatic one. Miss Baumgartner, my first grade teacher, was hard on me, making me do the same home-

First magazine subscription, 1957

work as everyone else. Under her tutelage I learned to read, one letter at a time. Then one word at a time. Finally, one sentence at a time, which is when I knew I had learned one of life's most powerful secrets: the secret of reading full sentences. It is, by any estimation, the pinnacle of reading.

A complete thought wrapped up in a string of words. It is a thing of elegance and beauty for the mind.

The next summer I read over 60 sentences. I kept a growing list of the sentences that I had read. I even joined a sentence club at school, where each child was given a sentence to read. And when I would dutifully turn in a sentence report, I always received the coveted gold star for my excellent ability to summarize the collection of words.

There is something magical about reading sentences, and this is something I try to pass on to the children that I speak to in the classrooms of our nation. I have been inspired by my mother, who has worked her whole life to promote what is called "literacy." Children need to discover that a whole new world opens up to them when they read an entire sentence. They can journey into a world of the head, in which ideas flourish, and new thoughts dawn.

My love of single lines of text continues to this day. If something important comes up, like a briefing or a policy paper or a bill, I am still able to absorb that entire first sentence. And I will surprise some of the members of my administration with how quickly I can read and comprehend that sentence and move on to the day's next scheduled activity.

In the demands and challenges of leadership, however, sometimes I do not have time to read an entire sentence, so I have learned to do what they call the "skimming" of sentences. I can skim just about any sentence and get the gist I want from it in minutes. This way I do not have to spend valuable time reading unnecessary words, and can focus my attention on governing the nation.

I have Miss Baumgartner to thank for that. I believe she is departed now, but I know that she can hear me in Heaven when I say thank you, Miss Baumgartner—or, I should say, Miss Butt-scratcher—for instilling in me a love of sentences. I am sure the American people thank you as well. Your good work inspired a President of history.

But just as important as learning to read was learning to interact with others socially, which is done through pranks.

One early instance of relating to others that formed my relating abilities involved a fellow classmate named "Ducky." One day, my friends and I felt that we had to teach Ducky a lesson, so we beat him up pretty good.

Then there was the day some of the gang and I tricked the math teacher, Mr. Phelks, into thinking his hearing aid was damaged. We did this by appearing to speak normally, but in fact whispering at a barely audible level.

After he was finished with his lesson, I went up to the front of the class as if I needed special help with the work, and I leaned in very close to his ear. I then blurted into his ear at the top of my lungs, "Mr. Phelks, I have a question about the assignment!"

He pretty near jumped out of his chair fumbling for the volume control on his hearing aid. I recall seeing a trickle of blood come out of his ear.

Another time, just as a lark, my friends and I burned down the school. No one of importance was hurt, I don't believe. Except the janitor, who slept on a cot in the boiler room. We cheered and hooted as we heard his desperate cries for help from behind the basement windows.

There is no question that I had a reputation for being sociable. We can look back now and laugh at all the folks who got hurt. But at the time, I found myself fighting against school officials who came down hard on me just for being myself.

In my numerous reports to my father, I cited countless interferences in my activities on the part of school officials, who would then face harsh rebuke.

I believe it is a serious matter when a school does not meet the needs of a school child. My school was woefully inadequate in meeting my needs. For example, when I stuffed a corncob down Stinky Delmar's pants in the lunchroom, I was cuffed repeatedly on the head. I do not believe this punishment fit the crime. When my friends and I stripped third grader Anthony Farsom naked and hung him by his ankles from the rafters of the gym during girls' volleyball practice, I was threatened with expulsion. This was wrong.

I lay the blame for my subsequent inability to meet my educational requirements squarely on Tim Horn, who alerted the hall monitor to my actions. Otherwise, it would not have been an issue and it would not have been a blot on my record.

Rest assured, Tim Horn faced justice on the playground.

However, there are many who deserve praise for their attention to my needs in school.

The person I idolized the most during my school years at Midland was my gym teacher, Mr. Fisher. If he witnessed any tomfoolery, he would administer "the Paddle." This was not the kind of loving punishment I would get from my mother's wood board. This was cold, calculating justice.

Mr. Fisher would make a boy grip the mesh lockers in

the center of the locker room without so much as an athletic supporter to shield his shame. He would ask him if he understood his punishment, and if the boy said "no" he would whack him on the behind. The sooner one could guess what he was being punished for, the sooner the paddling would end.

I learned that the people with the power know best. If the government could be run as Mr. Fisher ran his gym, the world might be free of horseplay.

When I was 13, my folks saw my potential for great educational privilege, and sent me away to the prestigious preparatorious academy, Phillips, in Andover, Maryland.

I was what they called "a gifted student" at Phillips Academy. I excelled in the areas of pushing and bullying fat kids, smashing eyeglasses, and putting tacks on chairs. I was proud of my achievements in these areas, as well as the high marks I received from other students in noogies, nipple twists, and the Indian-burn sciences. I was named Most Likely to Give a Wedgie by my classroom peers, two years running.

I continued to work to my strengths, and was later accepted to Yale on a full sucker-punching scholarship.

My favorite times at Phillips were the athletic events. I would admire the players running with the grace of a giraffe up and down the field. And I would admire more the boundless cheer of the cheerleaders, who would urge their team on no matter how far behind they were. Their enthusiasm was infectious. I resolved someday to become a cheerleader myself. It combined my two finest qualities, cheer and leadership.

Thus my formative young mind began to contemplate higher pursuits.

$$5$$

CAMPUS RADICAL

It was the height of the Vietnam War era. The campuses of our nation were alive with a heated debate, and an awakening of the political ideals of an entire generation of young people.

Many good folks disagreed on the issues. The students disagreed with the people. The people disagreed with the common man. And the African-American disagreed with our nation's laws concerning busses.

I took part in these great movements of social activistisms. Like many coloreds and youngsters of that time, I was out on the front lines of mass demonstrations of folks with my bullhorn, urging action to claim the victories we, the people, deserved.

My cause was the Yale Bulldogs, an organization

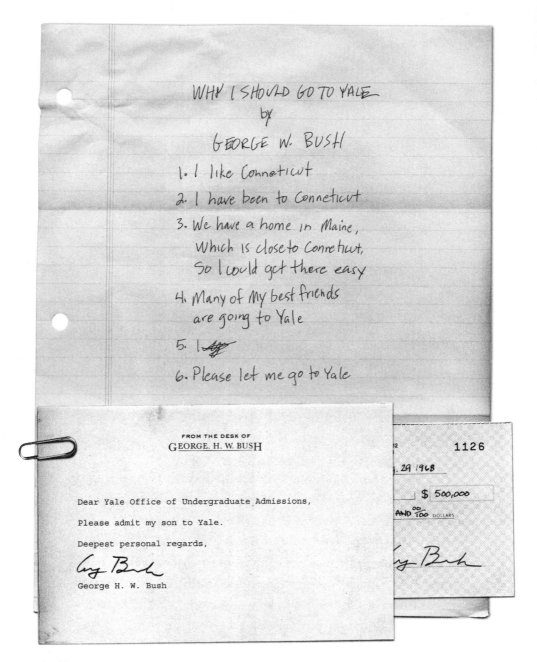

WHY I SHOULD GO TO YALE
by
GEORGE W. BUSH

1. I like Conneticut
2. I have been to Conneticut
3. We have a home in Maine, which is close to Conneticut, So I could get there easy
4. Many of My best friends are going to Yale
5. I
6. Please let me go to Yale

FROM THE DESK OF
GEORGE. H. W. BUSH

Dear Yale Office of Undergraduate Admissions,

Please admit my son to Yale.

Deepest personal regards,

George H. W. Bush

1126

29 1968

$ 500,000
AND 00/100 DOLLARS

College entrance essay, 1964

whose philosophy and goals I shared, passionately. The once proud 'Dogs were two in eight for that pivotal season of the mid-60s, and it was an injustice that they would continue to lose game after game, despite our hard work speaking out and making our voices heard.

But there were many who disagreed strongly with advocates like myself.

There was something in the air in those turbulent times. It was a time of great turbulence. What particular event moved me to cheerlead for the cause, I cannot say. Perhaps it was the loss of first-string running back Cal Barett, who sprained his ankle after the third game of that season and had to sit out crucial contests with Dartmouth and Harvard, costing us our rightful place in the finals. Perhaps it was a student body whose increasing indifference was evidenced by lower and lower attendance at the games. In their youthful complacency, they favored book-reading and studying over the important and timeless struggles taking place on the gridiron.

Or it could have been the special bond I felt with the struggling Yalie players.

It saddens the heart, the wrongs of the past. But whatever the reason, I had found my passion, and knew that I would fare well in the judgment of the history yearbooks.

I felt a special solidarity with the coloreds, who wanted only their fundamental right to be heard. I worked very hard to that end, calling out for everyone in the stands to yell as loud as they could. It did not make a difference what color you were. My cheers knew no racial boundaries. Though, to my memory, I am not certain if blacks were permitted at Yale Field in those days.

Whatever the winds that were blowing at the time, my blowing with them caused some friction in our family. My mother and father did not understand my activisting. My mother thought it "unmanly." I chalked that up to the intolerance of her generation. My father said nothing about it, but would only look at me with his forlorn, empty eyes when we met, our uneasy silence filling the room like a camel.

But still I continued my boundless cheer in the face of my parents' unacceptance and our team's defeats.

Being a leader of cheers was my priority at Yale. Nothing got in the way of that, not relationships, not sleep, and certainly not studies. I pursued it with a single-minded sense of purpose, like one does when he knows his cause is just.

I stayed up all night, and as other kids read politics and philosophy, I did the hard work of practicing new cheers for our team, and new taunts against the opposing teams. I lived for standing up in front of the ever-dwindling crowds at Yale Field, some of whom would protest the football games by booing, showing the ultimate disrespect for the players who fought for their school. This emboldened the enemy team. I refused to let them get away with it, cheering all the louder, calling back at them the "Boo who? Boo you!" retort cheer.

In those days we did not have the luxury of free speech zones where we could send those who disagreed with the reasoned chants of our cheer-squad. Dissenters had the right to express themselves directly on the sidelines. It was a truly chaotic time. We had to face their madness at every game. I believe in the end it helped build my resoluteness facing down these "squares" who would scorn our radical ways.

Hand-drawn war-rally poster, sophomore year at Yale, 1966

Our protestations did not end with home games, however.

I took what is known as "freedom rides" on busses with other radical students. We always took busses to away games, such as Brown, whose hardened ways and traditional values did not take kindly to our arrival in their town.

"Bulldogs, go home!" came one terrifying slur as we headed out of town on our freedom bus.

Once, our rivals even took to throwing eggs at our victory bus, almost striking me as I boarded.

There were other times when I feared for my very safety. But I was determined to remain strong in the face of their ignorance and hatred. I stood my ground, despite my fear of the opposing team's cheerleaders.

"We will crush you," came their oppressive words.

They went on, "We will C-R-U-S-H-U."

I dared not imagine the undoubtedly offensive meaning of this chant of random letters. One thing is for certain, it seared into my bones and introduced me to the fear I would one day see unleashed on America on September 11, 2001.

Was I ever in any danger? Perhaps. Being an outspoken supporter of the cause of both the Bulldogs and the celebrating of their successes consumed my every thought, and sometimes put me at great risk of bodily harm.

There was the incident with the beer and the fire hoses that got out of hand at the fraternity house. Some of my brothers were hurt, but thankfully, I escaped without serious injury.

But I was not afraid to risk arrest and jail time for my convictions. I received two warnings from Connecticut State troopers for what the authorities called "disruptive" behavior, one citation for loud noise disturbance at a fraternity party, and one arrest for driving while intoxicated.

I bore my persecution with pride, for I was fighting injustice against those who did not respect my fundamental freedoms. I stood up to the powers that be, and looked them in the eye, and said, "I defy your corrupt power structure to pass judgment on me." That is what I recall telling the court. But I do not remember exactly, as it was late at night, and I had been at a party, and it was very bright in the courtroom.

And though I could not see him through my haze, I suspect the judge looked back at me square in the eye and saw the steadfast resolve within me. I believe I earned his respect that night. I only had to spend one night in the county lock-up.

Another conviction for which I stood up and claimed my rights was that I should have access to the Kennebunk-port compound on weekends for lively gatherings. But my mom and dad disagreed. In the view of their generation, children had never been allowed to have parties at the compound.

But times were changing in the wind. This was a time when young people were rising up to challenge such outmoded conventions. And I stood with them.

I held many rallies at the compound. I encouraged many young people from college to join me in the struggle. It was a time to be free, and confront what some called the "bourgeois" or "privileged classes."

I held many sit-ins at the compound, reasoning that if my parents would not respect my viewpoint, I would not respect their rules, which were the vestiges of a bygone era of oppression and a violation of my rights.

We would often eat all their food and dance on their tabletops. We stood up against the privileged few by drinking their expensive wine, and sharing it with the many. Soon my parents could no longer deny the power of the people. They pulled the staff, and at the end of my Yale years, made extensive repairs to the property. They yielded to the forces of righteousness, and let us have our weekly late-night "Frat-Ins" at the compound for the duration of my time at Harvard Business School. The change my generation brought forth was here to stay.

Some look back on their radical college years and wonder, "Was I too radical?" Not me. I did something that mattered. I fought for Bulldog victory. And though it may not have been politically popular to cheer for the 'Dogs in those days, history has shown that they were an excellent team, consistently ranking in the top eight of the Ivy League.

While some were "AWOL" from the important struggles in this pivotal age, I am proud to have stood up when it counted, and lent my voice to this crucial era of our nation's collegiate football heritage.

6

FLYING HIGH!

I t was my destiny to be a war hero.

Though I did not think of it in these terms at that time. In the early days of Vietnam, I thought of military service as a duty. It was a duty to help the best I could to fight and defeat the enemy, and risk sacrificing up to two to three months of my life if necessary.

One thing is for certain, I did not think of it as a way to become a hero.

But a hero I would become, and it would be the decision of what kind of hero that I chose to be that was to shape history.

Every story of heroing has a beginning. When it came time to determine my course, I saw several paths before me.

I could be a sturdy Marine hero, saving my fellow soldiers from the fire of snipers and rats-nest attacks. But I was not the greatest of swimmers, so I rejected that course.

I could be a radio hero, radioing for help from the front whenever I saw fit. But there might be a lot of dials and wirings that could possibly confound my understanding, therefore I rejected that course as well.

Or I could be a potato-peeling or serving hero, wielding a large ladle to dispense much-needed sustenance to the troops, who would come one by one with their tin plates held out to me for food. And though I was strongly considered for this role by my superiors, medically I was unfit, having a life-long aversion to root vegetables and metal serving implements.

Any of these paths would have done my country honor. But in the end, I decided to be a flying hero. That way I could fly in the air.

It was a difficult time for our country—a time of war, for some. And I was fortunate to be selected for an elite fighting unit known as the "Champagne Corps" in the U.S. National Guard. The name was feared among the ranks of the enemy everywhere.

I joined this elite air unit in 1970. They immediately assigned me the important task of defending our nation's homeland. And I accepted. I was a soldier of the skies, ready to take orders and obey them without question. Up in the clouds, flying high.

Learning to fly was not an easy task. It took me two years before I was a qualified fighter pilot, yet surprisingly my service with the Guard would last just 14 months.

First they put me in a simulator, which back in those days was nothing more than a tin shack with a wooden chair and a broken broomstick, which I was asked to imagine was a throttle.

I am not good at imagining. I prefer reality, not the intangible mysteries of the mind's eye. So when I closed my eyes, I did not see the cockpit of a modern jet fighter. I saw a broken broomstick and a horseshoe hanging from the ceiling representing the yoke.

The heroes of those days were the test pilots: Commando Cody, Sky King, and the Rocketeer. They would often try to ease the tension and boredom in their lives by flying low and strafing the houses of their superior officers.

I wanted to emulate these exciting stunts, so when I went up on my first flight with my instructor, I jokingly suggested we strafe the Governor's mansion and give him a good scare. The instructor joked back, saying if I ever did that, I would be thrown in the brig for the duration of my service, and possibly tried for insubordination in a time of war. I laughed and laughed, but in the end, did not fly close to the Governor's mansion.

Texas and Alabama were rumored to be hotbeds of Communist insurgence in those times. By joining the Air National Guard, I was America's first line of defense against a direct attack on our shores. The mighty Vietnamese fleet could have lurked behind any cloud. Their feared bamboo squadrons terrorized the skies of the South.

I did not get much sleep in those days, forever worrying that at any moment the enemy might appear above, and I would be called upon to engage in an aerial duel—a dogfight where two men meet in flight, but only one man goes home and lands triumphantly. His opponent spirals to the earth uncontrollably, leaving a smoke trail in his wake, his chute not opening. Such are the stories of defeat.

One day in which I thought I might live out such a war scene was a hot and humid day in summer, 1972. The place: the swampy jungles of Alabama. The music: Jimi Hendrix.

I had to remain absolutely still. I wanted to move, to get under a tree for shade or to the brook for a drink of muddy water, but I knew that if I moved a muscle, a sniper might take me out. Every moment my life was at risk. This was the real nightmare my fellow soldiers and I lived when we golfed at the nearby Highland Park course.

So we hid in the trees. We became the trees. We were one with the forest so that the enemy could not see us. We lived, ate, and breathed the hell that infected our souls if we ever sliced into the rough.

Our socks were constantly damp, and thus foot fungus was a nagging problem for us fighting men in such primitive jungle conditions. Thankfully, the pharmacy in downtown Montgomery carried the name-brand athlete's foot creams.

The most harrowing adventure I experienced was like a scene from one of the finer war films that you have seen.

A select unit of my buddies and me—the elite of the elite—were chosen to go on a top-secret mission. Not even our commanders were to know the details. If we were captured, we would deny any knowledge of the plan. This was for the security not only of me and my men, but of the country, which we were charged with a sacred duty to protect.

We would commandeer Private Casey's El Dorado, and under the cover of night, drive across the state line to Tennessee. We would enter Nashville, to procure a precious bag of snow-white powder.

A6

Congressman's Son Single-Handedly Defeats Alabama-Based Vietcong
George Bush Jr. Awarded Numerous Medals For Bravery

HOUSTON, Aug. 13—George Bush Jr., son of Representative George Bush (R-Tex.), received a hero's welcome today when he returned home from the Alabama front after defeating the entire Vietcong force that had laid siege to the state of Alabama.

"I'm proud of my son. He's a pride-maker, this one, here," Rep. Bush said in a heartfelt letter upon greeting George Jr. at the Houston Airport for his public welcoming ceremony. The congressman was joined by wife Barbara Bush and dogs Bentley and Mrs. Fudsworth III. Houston mayor Louie Welch officiated.

A WAR HERO

George Jr. spoke at the brief ceremony, thanking those in attendance for their support and providing a rare glimpse into the realities of warfare.

"I faced a real enemy on a real field of battle," he said. "No one likes war. But the important thing is that I held my ground, and saved Alabama and perhaps our country from a very real threat."

Vietcong leader Ho Chi Minh is believed to have several guerilla fighters in the Alabama, Mississippi and Texas theaters. U.S. military commanders confronted this threat by establishing the National Guard's elite "Champagne Corps," which has tapped the sons of only the most influential political and business leaders. These bravest of the brave have been the first line of attack against the deadly east-Asian enemy storming our shores.

"The Vietcong did not have a chance against our fighting elite in Alabama," President Nixon said in a ceremony outside the White House Friday, during which he praised the National Guardsmen. The president singled out Bush in particular for his gallantry.

Houston Chronicle *article, August 13, 1973*

At 0300 hours we snuck out to embark on our mission.

We drove on for hours. I nearly fell asleep at the wheel at one point, near Birmingham.

My buddy Jim had to shake my shoulder and say, "George, come on! Remember why we are doing this!"

Of course, I did. We were doing it for the American people. I found a renewed strength deep within my heart, and continued onward.

Despite my fatigue and irritability, I knew it would all be relieved once we completed our mission.

We arrived in a motel on the outskirts of town at noon the next day. Salvatore, our contact, was waiting with a briefcase. It was all very clandestine. Was Salvatore CIA? We would never know. But the thrill of committed military service is something I have never forgotten. That is why, to this day, I deeply respect when others heed the call to serve.

We paid Salvatore with some cash I had procured, then I had the idea to go on alone. I sent my men back to the base in Montgomery, and I went on to complete even more risky secret missions in Connecticut and Kennebunkport. It might be months before my unit would see me again. These were off-the-record, secret blackbook missions which I am still not permitted to divulge in any detail.

But it was off the battlefield that times really got out of hand. My buddies and I knew how to celebrate. Like the test pilots of old, we would all meet at the bar after a tough day's piloting in the flight simulator and laugh and tell stories of combat.

This celebrating was an important part of the war effort. If we did not let loose the steam in the bar with fellow airmen, the pressure might be too much in the simulator the next day. Our pretend bombs might miss their imaginary targets, which would spell disaster for the make-believe ground troops. And the countless enemy guerillas, who only existed in our fantasies, would overrun the villages of Alabama and terrorize the made-up local folks—many of whom I had come to know as family.

Therefore it was imperative that we all stay out late and have many good times in those days, otherwise we might endanger the very innocents we swore to protect.

One time, after a particularly rugged night of dutiful celebrating, I was called up when one of the other pilots fell ill. I tried to claim illness also, but unfortunately the CO saw me out the night before and said, "If you can party, you can fly." So up I went. I had not slept at all, and the effects of my celebrating had not yet worn off. Fortunately, it was a four-hour fight, and by the end I was fast asleep, the instructor having taken care of the landing and much of the flying that preceded it.

I was flying high and proud, and getting some much needed rest.

There are some who have criticized my military service. In these pages I would like to take on these criticizers. I am proud to have served my country and protected its borders. When George W. Bush was patrolling the skies, more often than not the fate of the entire city of Tuscaloosa hung in the balance.

I say to my critics, let history be the judge of my legacy, not the historians.

History is written by the historical writers. And at present, I am writing the history. The historical criticalizers can write their critical historical writings, but I suspect that they will be dry and boring, full of dates, names, and facts. My history, by contrast, will captivate the discerning and patriotic reader.

After my service in the National Guard was complete, I experienced one of my proudest moments of the war.

It was in a private ceremony at my parents' home. My own father posed for a picture with me and pinned the prestigious "Son of a Congressman" medal on my uniform jacket. I was also awarded two Silver Spoons for bravery in a separate ceremony.

To think that my father, who himself had been killed in the Great War, would recognize my gallantry was a great honor. The flash of the bulb as we stood smiling together, my chest newly shiny with the medal, is one memory I shall never forget.

But an even prouder moment of public service, and the fulfillment of my destiny, would come many years later.

7

THEN I RAN SOME
COMPANIES INTO
THE GROUND

Avery important lesson taught at the Harvard Business School is the essential question one must ask when one is given the sacred trust to lead a corporation: "How can I quickly and efficiently run this company into the ground?"

It is this simple formula that is the key to financial success.

The cycle of a business is one of life and death, just like we see in nature. What the sciences of nature tell us is that sometimes the cycle is slower, like that of the red sequoia tree of the California woodlands, great giants which live for many weeks. On the other end of the spectrum is the small housefly, which only lives for a few short hours. Every company must close its doors at some point, and it is the CEO's job to see to it that investors earn a windfall profit.

Of course some will lose all of their money, but that is a pitfall of entrepreneurship. If the company has a capable CEO, he will lead the company to grow like the mighty redwood, and know how to recognize the exact moment at which to take a chain saw to it and get top dollar for the chopped wood.

The way the housefly fits into it all involves complicated business charts and formulas that we do not need to go into.

That is the sum total of the wisdom passed on at Harvard Business School.

After finishing in the top 300 in my class, I set out to put my training into practice. I would become an entrepreneur. My goal was to move back to Texas and succeed in a company that was in the business world.

And that is precisely what I set out to do.

I founded then sold some three or four companies in this period. Arbusto. Harken. Another one. And yet another, the name of which I cannot remember. Whatever the case, the companies all enjoyed successful tanking under my leadership.

One of the most important things about running a company is thinking of the name that that company will have. When I started a company, I chose a name which expressed the glorious flight of an eagle, or the burrowing majesty of the brave vole. If you knew the names, and if I could remember all of them for this work of history, you would like them, because a great deal of thought was put in to thinking up those names.

My first company, "Arbusto," would make our great

goal clear right in the name of the company. It was to be red ink or bust. And I worked hard to reach both of these goals by leading the company straight into the crapper.

First, I hired an incompetent staff who immediately set forth scheduling my vacations throughout the coming year.

This would not be an easy task.

Vacations sometimes conflicted with one another, and often overlapped. A special secretary had to be hired just

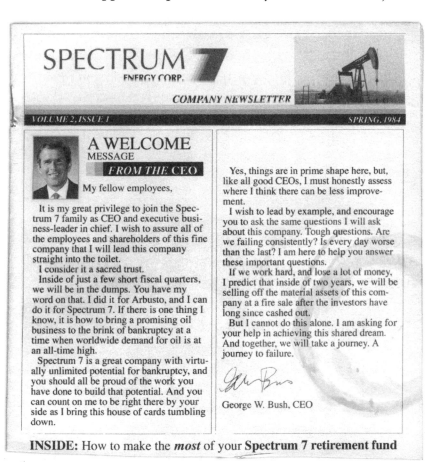

SPECTRUM 7
ENERGY CORP.
COMPANY NEWSLETTER

VOLUME 2, ISSUE 1   SPRING, 1984

A WELCOME
MESSAGE
FROM THE CEO

My fellow employees,

It is my great privilege to join the Spectrum 7 family as CEO and executive business-leader in chief. I wish to assure all of the employees and shareholders of this fine company that I will lead this company straight into the toilet.

I consider it a sacred trust.

Inside of just a few short fiscal quarters, we will be in the dumps. You have my word on that. I did it for Arbusto, and I can do it for Spectrum 7. If there is one thing I know, it is how to bring a promising oil business to the brink of bankruptcy at a time when worldwide demand for oil is at an all-time high.

Spectrum 7 is a great company with virtually unlimited potential for bankruptcy, and you should all be proud of the work you have done to build that potential. And you can count on me to be right there by your side as I bring this house of cards tumbling down.

Yes, things are in prime shape here, but, like all good CEOs, I must honestly assess where I think there can be less improvement.

I wish to lead by example, and encourage you to ask the same questions I will ask about this company. Tough questions. Are we failing consistently? Is every day worse than the last? I am here to help you answer these important questions.

If we work hard, and lose a lot of money, I predict that inside of two years, we will be selling off the material assets of this company at a fire sale after the investors have long since cashed out.

But I cannot do this alone. I am asking for your help in achieving this shared dream. And together, we will take a journey. A journey to failure.

George W. Bush, CEO

INSIDE: How to make the *most* of your **Spectrum 7 retirement fund**

Spectrum 7 company newsletter, 1984

to make sure that this did not happen. Once, when a long-awaited yachting vacation off the East Coast overlapped with a crucial fly-fishing trip back home, it nearly caused a disaster, putting at risk my plans for an important golf outing.

The 70s and 80s were an era of unbounded entrepreneurial spirit. And nowhere was that spirit reflected better than in the Texas oilfields. I learned from my father that to make money in oil, one must become an expert in the making of money with oil.

Oil futures, or paper oil, were very complicated transactings, related to the housefly business principle I addressed previously. But after a quick training period involving the signing of documents, the shaking of hands with investors introduced by my father, and joking around with the fellas in the company sauna, I took to it quickly.

Many golfing retreats took place during these years, as well.

Of course someone had to go out and find places to drill for oil. I left that to workers, the people within a company who do what is called the "work." I was the crucial Man in the Middle. And in this vital role, I would handle a slip of paper by placing it in various locations on my desk, laying it here for a week, then putting it over there. It was quite a thing to see how, over time, that paper would move.

To the untrained business eye, it looked as though Arbusto was doing quite well, and was not being run into the ground at all. But behind the scenes I worked hands-on, painstakingly neglecting the company every day, and eventually Arbusto collapsed like a superb house of cards.

And after all that successful failing, I would bid farewell to my good friends at Arbusto, waving as I exited into the Texas sunset, proud of all the good work I had undone.

After a short eight-month vacation, I hungered for another challenge. But that challenge would have to wait, since I had made the tough decision to extend my vacation another four months.

After feeling rested and refurbished, I set to work.

I was determined to achieve an even more catastrophic success at another company.

But first there was another crucial vacation that I had to take. This time to a Tibetan monastery where I would learn the ancient secrets of the mystics. Unfortunately, there were no four- or even three-star hotels there, so I went deep-sea fishing in the Florida Keys instead.

After this final vacation, I worked hard, building trust with my employees, bringing donuts to boost morale, sometimes with the tiny colored sprinkles on them for added cheer.

More importantly, I earned the trust of the board members. I set to work approving every measure that came before me. And before long we had amassed an enormous debt, for which I was understandably proud. One of the shareholders told me it was among the largest shortfalls he had ever seen.

My heart filled with pride at this compliment, but I wondered, could I do better still?

The name of my next company was either Bush Exploration or Spectrum 7. Regardless, through my bold and innovative management ideas, I would truly make a mark on the business world with this company. I would throw lavish dinners for investors. I would buy paper made from only the rarest trees deep in the African rainforest. I would invest in solid-gold paperclips, and platinum staples handcrafted by the best Swiss stapleteers.

Soon I was having many high-level meetings with foreign investors, to do what in business circles is called a "bail out." A true sign that one is a top performer in the marketplace.

Through some very skillful accounting, I drove this company into a spectacular hole, sold it for a fair price, and then watched as our lawyers triumphantly filed for Chapter 11.

I had done it again. I was beginning to get a reputation for my meteoric decline up the business ladder.

It was then that my secretary ushered in the man who would change my life forever. This mysterious acquaintance knew I had recently made a significant capital gain from the sale of company stock and was interested in a good investment, and he leaned over and gave me some very important advice. He said just one word.

"Rangers," he whispered.

"What?" I replied. "The Texas Rangers? Lawmen are not for sale. They are above the law."

"No," he said. "The Texas Rangers baseball team."

My eyes misted over.

Like most every young boy whose blood courses red with American veins, I dreamt of one day being a shareholder in a baseball franchise. I imagined giving the manager orders, telling him to make intuitive trades that would cost us the pennant year after year. I dreamt of leading the team in pre-game prayers that would touch the heart, and I dreamt of organizing public bonds to build new stadiums.

SPECTRUM 7
ENERGY CORP.

COMPANY NEWSLETTER

VOLUME 4, ISSUE 3   FALL, 1986

A FAREWELL
MESSAGE
FROM THE CEO

My fellow employees,

Years ago, I made a pledge. A pledge both to the stockholders and to myself. It was a promise to run this company into the ground. I am proud to announce that I have honored this commitment.

Today our company is fully insolvent. Our books are being pored over by teams of accountants, and they are shaking their heads at the sheer speed at which I have delivered this company to the creditors.

Such an impressive achievement cannot be accomplished by one man alone. I would like to take this opportunity to thank all of you who helped bring down our fine organization. I do not recall your names specifically, as I was rarely in the office, but I assure you that you have my deepest gratitude and appreciation for all the good work you did to manage this company's destruction.

I feel that my job here is done, so I have cashed out my shares and tendered my resignation. I leave you in the competent hands of the bank examiners. God bless you, and good luck.

George W. Bush, CEO

INSIDE: How to cash in your **Spectrum 7 retirement fund** for pennies on the dollar!

Spectrum 7 company newsletter, 1984

It was any boy's fantasy come to life.

Here was a company that I could run into the ground again and again, and it would continue to be bailed out by the city, county, state, or whichever regulatory body was responsible for keeping the team in its hometown. I had stumbled upon what is known in business as the perfect company.

We would charge a fair price for tickets, and the fans would buy them. Great losses would come from an antiquated stadium that was difficult to renovate into the modern age. So we would build a new stadium. Our losses would multiply even further. And soon the new stadium would become outdated.

The cycle of natural business life would begin again. It was a golden, no-win situation. I was in my element.

I remain grateful to the hard-working taxpayers of Texas who helped me reach my potential with the Texas Rangers. They believed I could deliver the overruns, and I did.

My experience on the baseball diamond was the high point of my business career, the last step in a string of cataclysmic accomplishments of which I could be deeply proud. But fate would ultimately guide me to a test of kingly proportions: managing not just a company, but a whole state, and eventually a country.

It was to be an awesome responsibility, one for which my experiences in both business and frog-torture had prepared me.

8

THE CLOWN-FACED ZOMBIE
I CALL MY WIFE

When a man reaches a certain age, he feels an urge to settle for the closest woman around who seems interested. He then embarks upon one of the most rewarding periods of life.

I was blessed with the good fortune of meeting a wonderful small-town Texas woman who had a dazed and clueless stare reminiscent of a goat that had been struck between the eyes with a tire iron—a halting kind of beauty which every man desires in a woman.

It was at a backyard barbecue of mutual friends. The midday Texas sun shone brightly. Laura was gnawing at meat with her make-up-caked face, much like the majestic condor might tug at the cartilage of a road-kill skunk. I watched enraptured as she devoured the ground flesh while slurping lemonade, putting bright red stamps of lipstick on her plastic cup.

When she wasn't shoving sustenance into her mouth, she was tenderly nursing a cigarette butt. Its hazy fumes softened the sun's glare, creating a smoggy halo effect which enhanced her angelic visage.

Her frozen look of wide-eyed terror combined with her unwavering open-mouth smile captivated my senses. As if through an expensive embalming, a permanent, silent shriek had been fused to her skull.

I felt compelled to start a conversation with this picture of elegant refinement. I soon realized that she had a vibrant and alert personality to match her fierce instinct for scavenging the meat of lesser beasts.

We began spending a great deal of time together.

I eventually found that her enchanting stupor was the result of inhaling—and, at times, ingesting—copious amounts of chemically active make-up compounds, which at the time had not been properly tested on monkeys in order to ensure that they would not cause crippling side effects.

Furthermore, Laura could not get through an hour— let alone a day—without grasping for a cigarette. It was like was her oxygen line. A captivating charm came over her as she sucked the cool, fresh nicotine into her lungs. Knowing that her teeth were yellow with tobacco stains, the inside of her mouth coated in a viscous, carbon-monoxide film, and her lungs black with soot, only made her more radiant.

She employed all manner of dyed clays and advanced plasters and paints to keep the tobacco-stained stumps of rotting bone in her yap shining lovely and white. The dreamy cloud of smoke that hovered about her wherever she went cured her skin much like the hide-tanning process, which served to make her skin more durable and tough.

That Laura was a horrendous beauty is beyond doubt. But what I must frequently remind myself is that her mind is important to me as well.

In her early years, before we met, she had undergone extensive social and attitude conditioning at the Midland Woman's Society, which was funded by the Midland Husband's Society. She was therefore a well-tutored woman, one whom any man would be happy to call his wife.

We are the same age, Laura and me, although when we met, she seemed much older. This seeming age difference did not affect our interactions. She had a fetching burlap-

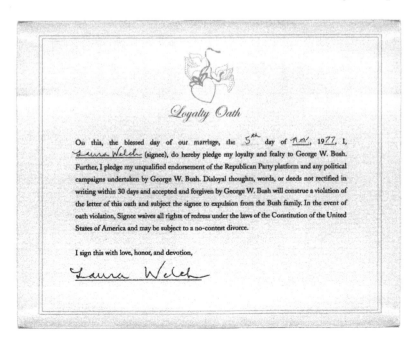

Loyalty oath signed by Laura Welch, 1977

like complexion, a fuddy-duddy countenance that made my heart go pitter-patter. And she wore a long dress that draped her frumpy form like a tarp over grass seed.

She was a bewitching woman, like a queen hag from a magical Halloween storybook. At that time, I would later learn, she undertook great effort to de-agify her face, using colored powders, creams, and paints. Today, add to that list the occasional doctor's visit.

She looks quite good for a 60-year-old, which I believe is her age at the time of this writing. And her hair gains a new luster with professional-strength dyes, stiffening agents, and toxic sprays. But her lovely half-smile, paralyzed as if in permanent fear, beams with a radiance that can only come from her tough cheek skin being pulled, stretched, and pinned back.

She also has undergone a major frownoplasty, a complicated and delicate surgical procedure which removes the frown-inducing muscles around the jawbones, cheeks and eye sockets.

But that is enough compliments!

Our whirlwind courtship was one of passion, but also convenience. We were both over 30 when we met, and the time to start a family was in danger of passing us by. We discussed the matter, and decided that we wanted children so that Laura's eerie grin and chicken eyes might live on through the mystifying science of insemination.

She especially wanted daughters to whom she could pass on her tradition of womanhood. She yearned to teach a litter of piglets to apply expensive fragrances, so that they would grow up to emit a sweet, pungent odor of some kind of scented plant or chemically re-engineered whale oil.

The only danger in this plan was that these young children would send off a sickly sweet aroma so strong that they might be sought out and eaten alive by ants. This fear has come perilously close to reality several times, and I have spent a great deal of money insulating our homes over the years with weather-resistant poison granules, buckets of ant gel, sticky traps, and other extermination methods to keep the ants at bay.

But despite the risk, we knew that we wanted a family.

Our wedding was a traditional Texas one, held in a small Methodist church in Midland. The reception was an old-fashioned Texas barbecue, with the country band "Whispering Tumbleweeds" playing. I celebrated in another proud Texas tradition, the one in which a great deal of drinks are served.

During our first dance, Laura looked at me with her empty red eyes, and reminded me of my promises to her. She whispered tenderly into my ear "I will eat your soul." I smiled at her and said, "You are my clown-faced zombie, now and forever." And our covenant of love was sealed.

In the intervening years, I watched as Laura allocated a good percentage of her allowance to make-up and perfume costs. She ordered it in bulk quantities directly from manufacturers. Her rouge budget alone approached that of a small city government in those early months, as did the money spent for exotic ointments, industrial balms, and facial enamels.

Surgically, there were several options available to her, all costly, but in the end worth the money, for they would capture her expensive facial construction for all times. She opted for a living mummification procedure. This would replace the blood with a unique combination of rare formaldehydes, slowing any deterioration of the smile or any smile-related tendons, which might fatigue with age. This taxidermy left her with a strange odor, and a texture to her skin not unlike that of a sack of cattle feed, but did not impede her ability to walk and wave under her own power.

And I thought she was lovely.

I wish to stress at this point that I believe women have a prominent role to play in our society. When I discovered I was to be the father of twin girls—double the trouble!—I knew there would be a great deal of unwelcome smells and squawking debates within the home. When my daughters were born, I realized I would have to keep my guard up around this putrid family of bellowing hyenas which I had inadvertently spawned.

I also knew I was the luckiest man in the world.

It was to be a lot of work keeping these precious glaze-

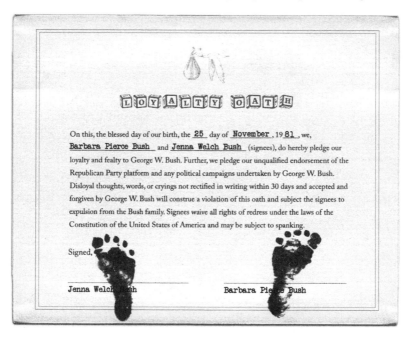

Loyalty oath signed by daughters Jenna and Barbara, 1981

eyed bitties under control. But though I put on a stern face with them, and grew practiced at putting my foot down, I was truly pleased to have so many yapping bird-faces in my life, each one encaked with a thicker frosting of eye, lip, and cheek paint than the next, and each cloaked in a dense fog of flowery body-odor suppressants.

Laura became queen of the goblins at home. She lorded over our squealing, stable family. The house was always impeccable, as she was an expert at frightening the servants into doing a good job with their household duties, and at smiling silently at our young girls until they were creeped into doing what she had asked.

I always had a meal waiting for me when I returned home from a vacation, no matter what time of day. And she took good care of my feet, massaging them and loofahing the calluses away. My feet are tender and beautiful even today, thanks to Laura's expert care. In return I would pamper her with trips back to her ancient Egyptian doctor for frequent re-mummification, to keep her skin nice, dry and taut so that the make-up would seep in, like latex exterior house paint on old wood.

I place a great deal of value on the woman's perspective, when it is expressed appropriately. Laura is always there to offer her unconditional support for whatever I am doing. On occasions when I must watch her stiffly attempt to speak, her surgically stretched mouth barely able to deviate from its meticulously carved smile, I swell with pride and devotion.

She is more than just a life partner to me. She is an ever-present and terrifying force in my life's journey.

Surely, I have been blessed by the Almighty.

9

GEORGE W. BUSH, CONGRESSMAN FROM TEXAS'S 19TH DISTRICT— GOT A NICE RING TO IT!

This, I will admit, is one of the more boring chapters of my book. I encourage you to turn to a chapter that tells of some of my life's more exciting victories. Or perhaps you could read a magazine or watch television. There is no reason to read this particular chapter.

It is a complicated undertaking when one journeys into the mind's past to uncover what one was thinking when one decided to run for a small political office and proceed to lose handily. Many have said that I was not cut out for the U.S. Congress. Still others contend that the circumstance of my Connecticut birth prejudiced the good voters of Texas against my political campaign. But there is no doubt in my mind as to what event conspired to cost me that election: A werewolf curse.

A heartless half-man, half-wolf monster lurked on the dark plains of Midland, Texas in those days, and many local citizens would hear his bloodcurdling howls during the nights. I suspect the meaning behind his angry cries was simple—he did not want George W. Bush to represent the 19th District.

One dark evening as I came home from campaigning, I climbed out of my car only to see two dots of light in the distance. It was the searing eyes of the bloodthirsty werewolf. Or possibly it was the headlights of an oncoming automobile, which coincidentally passed that spot a few moments later. But to this day I believe it was a werewolf.

These facts raise a troubling question: Why were werewolves set against my becoming a member of Congress? After reflection, I am convinced that it was my strong anti-wolf stance. I had pledged to be tough on wolves. I made it clear that I was against moon-based transformations from man into beast. I also fought vigorously against regulating the sales of silver bullets at gun shows.

I knew that this would not win me any friends in the werewolf community. But I did not set out to become a U.S. Congressman in order to win a popularity contest. I set out to become a U.S. Congressman to hunt down and kill werewolves.

Werewolves aside, let me go back a while and reflect on what had led me to this race initially. It was 1978. Everyone had a pet rock and a mood ring and a jogging suit in those days. But for me, what compelled me to run for a seat in the House of Representatives was my involvement in two important failures. One, I had helped conduct my dad's two unsuccessful bids for a Senate seat several years earlier. Two, I had helped conduct my dad's second unsuccessful bid for a Senate seat, which I just mentioned.

After such valuable experience losing political contests, I knew that if I directed my energies toward my own campaign for Congress, there was a good possibility I, too, would enjoy some of this lack of success.

We initially conducted a poll among a small sample of my strongest supporters to get a feel for what the people would expect from a State Representative George W. Bush.

The first question was, "How much will you donate to the George W. Bush campaign for Congress?" Overwhelmingly, the answer was "How much do you need?" The follow-up survey question was, "If indeed you did donate to the George W. Bush campaign for Congress, who would you make out the check to?" Again, overwhelmingly, the answer was "George W. Bush." I was thrilled.

We surveyed three people for the poll: My father, the Emir of Bahrain, and Sheik Hassu Bin-Laden.

I learned a valuable fact from this survey: My dad had access to a great deal of money. It is a life lesson I have carried with me, and which has brought me comfort in times of trial.

But I am not the kind of person who listens to polls or surveys to make my decisions. I had a great deal of experience running unsuccessful political campaigns, and therefore had already learned the number-one lesson: In order to win, a candidate must go from town to town and shake the hand of every voter in the district and say "My name is George W. Bush, and I am asking for your support in my run for Congress." It is that simple.

I said this key phrase many, many times on the campaign trail. I said it so many times and to so many people, I sincerely believe I began saying it in my sleep. I would say it at other inappropriate times as well. At the breakfast table, Laura would ask if I would like more flapjacks and I would say, "My name is George W. Bush, and I am asking for your support in my run for Congress." I would catch the dog relieving himself where he was not allowed, and I would hit him on the nose with a rolled-up newspaper, shake my finger, and yell, "My name is George W. Bush, and I am asking for your support in my run for Congress!"

Therefore, as one can clearly see, this is a technique of campaigning that can wear on a candidate, because of the great strain of rememborizing a phrase that is involved.

There must be a better way to run a political campaign, I thought. Sadly, by the time I had this important insight, the election had already happened and I had lost.

The intricacies of political campaigns and races are many. And they have the effect, sometimes, of confounding one's brain capacity for rational thinking.

I was lucky to have a skilled and capable staff who ran my campaign. They were, in total, my wife, my 1974 Dodge Dart, and our dog, Hokum.

My campaign slogan, which Laura helped me write, was "Vote George W. Bush, He is not from Connecticut." It was an excellent slogan, and it garnered me many votes that I suspect otherwise would have gone to my opponent if I had not had such an outstanding slogan.

Laura was by my side for most of the campaign. After her most recent embalming, she did not require nutritional sustenance of any kind, so we put in the long hours.

George Bush: Not From Connecticut

ON NOVEMBER 7,
VOTE FOR WEST TEXAS.
VOTE FOR
George Bush for Congress

Dear Voters,

Laura and I would like to take this opportunity to remind you that I am not from Connecticut. I spent some of my life right here in Texas.

While meeting many of you on your ranches or at your barbecues, I hope you have had a chance to hear my important message: that I was not born in Connecticut, nor did I attend expensive private schools there.

Your thoughts on the issues facing West Texas are my primary concern. Most importantly, I want you to know that I am just like you, and not a Yale-educated blue-blood from a powerful political family with deep ties to the East Coast elite.

As we approach Election Day, I urge you to consider my vision for Texas. A bold vision unlike anything relating to Connecticut, where I am not from.

Thank you,

Campaign poster from Texas 19th-district
Congressional race, 1986

She would simply sit at my side, or stand, if standing was called for, in her pants suit, expressing her support for my campaign. She typically would not put in a good word, due to the physical difficulty it posed. She would, however, clap enthusiastically at my speeches, which could be painful for her, as brittle skin and bones can sometimes shatter when slammed together in a clapping motion. But she was a trouper, and took that risk.

Laura and I both believed strongly in the importance of running a clean campaign. My opponent, whose name I cannot recall, was a fine opponent. I did not dwell on the fact that he had had sex with a sow earlier in his youth. What he did with a pig at one time was his own affair, and, in my mind, had no bearing on how well he would serve the people of the 19th district. Voters should consider the issues, not the fact that he made more trips to the barn for secret rendezvous with a breeding hog than he did to his own marital bed. I made it very clear in my campaign literature that this was his private lifestyle, and not an appropriate issue for voters to be concerned about.

On the campaign trail, the men and women of West Texas voiced skepticism about my campaign, and sometimes became disagreeable when I spoke. Babies, on the other hand, smiled and cooed when I held them for the cameras. Furthermore, they seemed compelled by my ideas. As the campaign wore on, I began to prefer campaign events with fewer and fewer adult voters, and more and more infants. I spoke at day-care centers and hospital maternity wards. I shook a lot of tiny little hands in bassinets, through the bars of cribs, and in carriages on the street. These were places where my message was resonating.

As Election Day dawned, I was optimistic. Unfortunately, I discovered on election night that babies do not have the right to vote in this country. This was an injustice that I pledged to one day rectify.

Regardless of the outcome, I believed my campaign for Congress was a successful one. I raised many vital issues of our time which I believed mattered to the voters in my district. The werewolf issue, for one. Another one of my signature issues was the urgent need to get George W. Bush sitting in one of those wooden chairs at the U.S. House of Representatives. I knew these views would not make me the most popular person in West Texas, but I stood up for what I believed in my heart.

In the end it was a triumph. The Election Day party lasted all night. And even though we lost the popular vote, I believe that if there had been an electoral college, and the results had been contested, and it had gone all the way to the Supreme Court to straighten it out, we would have won handily.

I tucked myself into bed that night and thought of all the new friends I had met during my campaign. I credit my successful defeat to those good folks who would become, some 15 years into the future, an integral part of my race for Governor of the largest state in our nation. Or one of the largest, I believe. If Alaska is not counted.

10

MY NAME IS
GEORGE W. BUSH AND I AM
NOT AN ALCOHOLIC

It was on the occasion of my 40th birthday that I had to make a tough choice, and face the facts.

Much has been made of my tendency to celebrate a bit too much. And I admit that, at one time, I enjoyed life.

Life is better when you can "tie one on," and be with friends. And socializing in this way makes having friends much easier. If you do not like them, for example, a little sip now and then helps increase one's tolerance level for such people.

I was happy when I was socializing, having the occasional celebratory drink. I saw things through a pleasant haze, like I was looking through sheer curtains. On the other side of those curtains was a happy place where everyone was my friend, and good times were enjoyed.

By contrast, on occasions when I was not in a social state, tempers tended to flare more easily. This can be a positive thing for a President, such as in times of war, when one must fight.

For a businessman, it can mean the success or failure of a company. Particularly for people-oriented businesses like the ones I ran into the ground. And if I was to be destined to push those companies into the stratospheres of bankruptcy, I would be sure to do it by over-celebrating.

During one memorable incident when I was in high school, I drank some Texas Firewater straight from a bootleg still operated by a classmate. The next thing I remember after that long night of the sweet burning liquid was waking up two days later. My friends said that I had slipped into unconsciousness, so they put me behind some shrubs in the back yard to sleep it off.

I learned later that it was probably what doctors call an alcohol-poison-induced coma, and that I might have suffered some brain damage to my mind as a result.

Fortunately for our country, it is clear that this was not the case.

In another instance I awoke in the bed of a pickup truck somewhere, and did not know where I was. Eventually, through the use of deducting, I was able to discern by the make and model of the pickup, the license plate, and the driveway that it was parked in, that I was on my own property.

But after forty years of this kind of good cheer, and an inclination to toast in times of triumph, it was time to face the hard truth: I did not have a drinking problem.

And this, the occasion of my 40th birthday, was definitely not the time to take responsibility for this absence of a problem.

Those whom I was closest to had brought my lack of a drinking problem to my attention previously. One friend in particular, my good friend Fred, had taken me aside one night after a lot of good times and said, "George, seriously, how about another one?"

I had reached the age when one must acknowledge the cold hard reality. And the reality of this situation was that Angels had a grand destiny planned for me, and the fact that I could hold my liquor just fine did not figure into those plans.

The day I realized that I was not an alcoholic changed my life.

The first and most important thing I realized about my lack of a drinking problem was that I did not need any help. Alcoholism is a serious disease, I have learned, and it requires serious treatment. There was no doubt in my mind that I did not need such treatment, since I did not have the disease.

I knew that I must not only forgo treatment, but I had to look past any of the root causes. And one thing was certain: I did not have to face the various inner demons that I was not keeping at bay through an occasional drink.

I informed my doctor about my lack of concerns about this non-issue. He did not put me in touch with Alcoholics Anonymous, where, if you join, unlike me, you go to a meeting where you get a sponsor who is a recovering alcoholic. The sponsor knows the pitfalls of giving up drinking. Only a personal sponsor can give an alcoholic the help he needs, and see him through the tumultuous turmoil of the first few days of being clean and sober.

This, obviously, was not my experience.

I never had an AA sponsor, and he was in no way named Al—"Big Al" is what I never once called him. He did not bring me to my first AA meeting, where I failed to learn the 12 steps. I am not aware of these 12 steps, nor did I learn of them that night.

At this particular meeting, which I did not attend, I did not stand up and introduce myself, saying, "I am George W. Bush, and I am not an alcoholic."

The people there did not think to respond supportively by saying "Hi George," because, as I said, I was not there. I did not pour out my soul to this group of strangers, breaking down and sobbing, nor did I curl up in a fetal position on the floor of the VFW, where the meeting was not held.

To the contrary, I continued to enjoy my life during this period, as I knew there was nothing wrong.

I also successfully faced the reality of not needing to go to rehab. Since I did not have a drinking problem, I knew I could lick this lack of a problem myself quite easily. And I did.

After I made the decision to not quit not drinking, or in other words, not not have a lack of a drinking problem anymore, I knew without a doubt that I would not become what they call a "dry drunk" for the remainder of my days, and thus there was no possibility that I would begin to act out my frustrations on everyone else.

It was a liberating experience to finally not admit my weaknesses, and not ask anyone for help.

Since that day, the years have been ones of crystal clarity.

But there have not been times of temptation.

I had no moment of weakness in 1988. My father had been elected President of the United States, and there was a gathering with all my very best friends in attendance. Champagne was everywhere. A full flute was presented to me on a silver platter by a passing server. My hand in no way trembled or hesitated as it reached for the comforting medicine. My mind did not replay the epic struggle of what I had not been through. A very important life decision was not put before me. One that I knew I would not have to confront day in and day out for the rest of my life. There was no inner battle, raging through my soul like a tornado exposing my every self-doubt.

I had a wonderful time at this party, and at no time enjoyed the excellent champagne.

Today, as I continue to never face down this nonexistent day-to-day struggle, I always remember the very special someone who helped me.

Every day in my prayers I thank Jesus for helping me realize that without proper treatment, there was a good chance that I could live a normal and productive life, and I would not suffer any symptoms of untreated alcoholism, because I had the best treatment of all: Angels.

Jesus and His hosts grant me the willpower to deal with this non-situation on my own, and the fact that I continue to live a full and happy life in which denial plays no part.

At eight months, February, 1947

2

Enjoying a wash-basin bath in 1948

3

Christmas at home, 1950

Learning to ride a tricycle at age 3, 1949

On the oil fields of Texas, 1956

6

On the Yale baseball field, 1965

Texas Air National Guard, 1972

7

Training in the Air National Guard, 1972

Receiving Lieutenant stripes, 1973

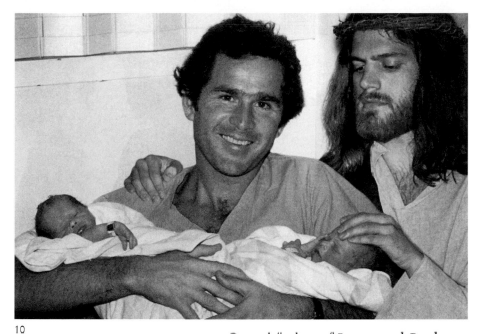

10

Proud father of Jenna and Barbara,
November 25, 1981

11

On the campaign trail during the 1978 race for the
19th Congressional District of Texas

12

1992 family vacation to the Grand Canyon

*With daughter
Jenna at a 1984
campaign rally for
President Ronald
Reagan*

13

14

Supporting the Texas Rangers baseball franchise, 1997

Inauguration as 43rd President of the United States,
January 22, 2001

Speaking to troops at Fort Carson, CO, 2003

Returning from a surprise visit to the troops in Iraq, 2003

Working in the Oval Office, 2002

19

*Rallying rescue workers at Ground Zero,
September 14, 2001*

20

2002 State of the Union address

Departing for G-8 Summit, 2004

22

*Surveying the aftermath of Hurricane Katrina
from Air Force One, August 31, 2005*

23

*Oval Office meeting with senior advisors,
March, 2006*

Mission Accomplished, May 1, 2003

11

THE GREATEST LOVE OF
MY LIFE: JESUS

The first time I opened a Bible was an auspicious occasion.

It was in the mid to late 1980s at my parents' home, which at that time was the official residence of the Vice President of the United States of America in Washington. In this stately mansion of rulers they had on display the beautiful Bush family Bible. It had ornate engraving on the cover, and stood on a pedestal in an honored place in the library.

They had received the cherished volume as a gift from the celebrated prophet Billy Graham, a Godly man and frequent dinner guest of our family. He looked like a frank-incensed Wise Man from the days of the Hebrew Kings. His piercing eyes had the effect of searing right through a person, like holy lasers. The Rev. Graham looked at me as though he had the power to call on God to strike me down if I was found wanting.

Therefore, I tended to avoid those particular family dinners whenever possible.

Because this particular Bible had originally come from such a prominent TV holy man, I believe there is a possibility that the book had some special powers to project prayerfulness. Perhaps God had added more "Jesus dust" to this particular edition, as a personal favor to His good friend, the Rev. Graham.

I will be honest and admit that it was a difficult book to read. It was a very large book, but the words within it were printed very small. The pages were a delicate kind of tissue-like rice paper that crumpled and tore apart as I flipped through the book, quickly skimming over the boring parts.

It appeared to start at the beginning, I noted — the beginning of everything. All the knowledge that man has accumulated since the Times of the Giants. It was truly a breathtaking work of sacred writing.

I did not get far in the book. I merely glanced at some of the decorative letters at the start of the chapters, and marveled at the religiosity of the printing and binding.

The first sentence in the book is a riddle that continues to confound the philosophers of men.

But I am getting ahead of myself.

Jesus did not touch me at this time. This was simply my first meaningful introduction to the Good Book.

I had known about the Bible before that. Long ago. I had known about religion from Sunday School. But I did not know much about Jesus himself. And what I did know of Him, I did not particularly like, what with His funny sayings and His raggedy clothes. He seemed like a dirty and foul person who appealed mostly to what were known in those days as "the hippies," or "the Jesus freaks." Besides all that, I was what some would have called a "sinner" who enjoyed good times. What did I need, I thought, with someone like Jesus who would save me from all the fun?

But then came the night in Washington, where I glanced at that Bible and saw the biblical trimmings on the grand book, and heard the Jesusy tones roll out from the lordly mouth of Billy Graham. Something stirred inside of me. But I did not know what.

After that evening, I knew I wanted the stirring to continue.

Upon my return home to Texas, I joined a men's Bible study group. They met every Wednesday in the conference room of the Houston Hyatt. With a group Bible study, I reasoned, the men would assemble and discuss Biblical teachings in a setting more like a cocktail party than a dull classroom, safeguarding me from having to slog through the whole book.

In a side note, I want to point out that the "modus operandi" above has since become a central part of my leadership strategy. I find the experts, let them tell me what I need to know, then take action. It is easier for me to make decisions when I am not burdened by irrelevant facts that complicate my thinking. In the instance of the Bible study group, the other men shared with me their view of the facts, which was that I should give my heart to Jesus.

It happened right there in the Bible study meeting.

I looked up from a conversation I was having with some of the other men, and there He was, standing there, on the other side of the crowded room, smiling at me. Our eyes locked, and it was an instant, unbreakable connection.

I felt my heart skip a beat, as they say. I examined Him closely. He wore a tattered rag-like robe. His skin was a slightly darker hue, like that of the East Indian or the mulatto. And He had a face like that of the movie star Mel Gibson, but more Jewishy.

He tucked His flowing, golden-brown hair behind His ear as He knelt down to help an injured lamb. At first I was surprised that there was a wounded farm animal in the hotel conference room, but I was touched and filled with great rejoicing when He touched the lamb with a magical healing energy to mend the creature's broken leg. The goat ran free, into a field of flowers.

Jesus then stood and walked over to me, and He said, "Give all you have to the poor and follow me."

I got a good chuckle out of His comment, and looked behind me to see if He was addressing someone else.

As He stood there, staring intently at me, my second thought was to call hotel security. I did not know, in those days, if Jews were permitted in the Houston Hyatt.

But Jesus had a soothing quality about Him which made me forget about the laws of men. Was this a vision I was having? Perhaps I had had too much to drink, I wondered.

I responded to Him by saying the first thing that came to my mind, "Hello, Jesus, my name is George W. Bush, and I am asking for your support in my run for Congress." Then I extended my hand to Him. Though His handshake was limp, like a woman's, I nonetheless felt a tingle of excitement as He took my hand.

He looked at me like He did not understand what I was saying.

To make a long story short, we began talking. I told Him what I planned to do for the people of West Texas. I recall going into a significant amount of detail on my position on werewolves, a spiel which usually held the ranchers spellbound.

But Jesus seemed above such earthly concerns. That night, we stayed up late talking about scripture, political philosophy, and the possibility of God putting out a one-sheet Bible summary.

I found I agreed with everything that Jesus said.

Jesus was the Prince of Peace, and I too believe in peace first and foremost. War is a last, desperate option to be used only when diplomacy fails to achieve the military objective of total annihilation of the enemy.

Jesus also cared deeply for the lowest of the low, and so do I. I believe in tax relief for Wal-Mart and other large department store chains, which clothe and feed the poor.

Jesus associated with the prostitutes and the beggars and the reviled of society, and those are the same kinds of people I associate with, as well.

I especially agreed with the part about eternal life. If you simply accept Jesus as your personal savior, all sins are wiped clean. It is all automatic. There is no memorization. No forms to sign. No outlay of capital. You just say "Jesus, come into my heart," and He takes you. It is that simple.

From that day forward, I have had Jesus in my heart. And I know that He will guide my soul to Heaven after I die, so therefore it does not matter what else I do in life.

Jesus has taught me that the material things of man are an empty promise compared to the rewards of the Hereafter, which to my understanding involves a great deal of light, harp music, and warm sensations of some kind.

But there was a dark cloud on the horizon concerning my new relationship with Jesus, one we both knew we would have to confront one day. I was betrothed to another. And I could not give my heart to two people. I am speaking of my relationship with my invisible friend, Mr. Bigsby, who had been with me since I was 4 years old.

I continued to promise Jesus that I would give my heart fully to Him, and that I would leave Mr. Bigsby at the appropriate time. It was difficult for me. Mr. Bigsby and I had been through a lot together. The bedwetting years. Comforting me when I got in trouble for killing my pet weasel. His warmth, kindness, and wacky laugh had kept me company and provided me with an ideal playmate through the loneliest days of my youth.

I did not wish to hurt Mr. Bigsby, and I know this is not a nice thing to say, but I had outgrown him. More and more lately I found I was not laughing at his jokes. I grew less and less excited about playing "tired fireman," "pin the frog," or any of the other games we used to play.

I broke the difficult news to Mr. Bigsby, in the closet of my bedroom, where we typically met. He got very angry. He yelled, stamped his big clown feet, and cried like a baby. I told him that if he wanted to be my friend, he would have to respect my decision to be with Jesus. Turns out, Mr. Bigsby was not a very good friend after all. He left and never came back. I still miss him and his silly antics, but he was emotionally distant, and it was not a healthy relationship. I am much happier with Jesus.

At first, things were all rosy with Jesus. I followed His advice to the letter, and gave all my money to the poor. I wore tattered robes and sandals, just like the Lord, and wandered the countryside, homeless, preaching to those who would listen. Many of my colleagues in business and politics wondered if I had lost my mind. I filed for chapter eleven and Laura and I lost the house. Our daughters were furious.

After I got arrested and thrown in jail for vagrancy, I decided that I did not want to live like that anymore. So I selflessly renounced all of my previous renunciations, and took back all my money from the poor.

I chalk up that whole experience to the over-eagerness one feels in the initial stages of a relationship.

One area in which Jesus has helped me greatly is in the area of my enjoying a good time, and having a few after-dinner drinks. Jesus told me the Jack and Cokes were wrong, and I listened.

However, I find it an interesting contrast that He is always there with the wine. Sometimes He just keeps pouring and pouring, and it seems as if He has a bottomless bottle of wine at His disposal. And when He does not have any wine, He turns tap water into wine.

Jesus' love of wine has been a problem in our relationship. Despite the fact that He had asked me to cut down my drinking, He continued to offer me the wine. On many occasions He has tempted me by turning O'Doul's into wine. I ask Him nicely to stop, but it is one of His miracles, and I must accept it as a holy occasion and drink up.

But no relationship is without its troubles. A relationship takes work, and Jesus and I must work on our problems together.

The hard work of prayer is just such an example. Perhaps you know how it can be in a long-term relationship after the initial excitement has died down. Prayer is still the cornerstone of my relationship with Jesus, make no mistake. But it is not the inspired spiritual experience like it was in the beginning. We still pray twice a day, maybe three, even though we have been together for 20 years. Sometimes we will even bring in Laura to pray with us, to spice things up a bit.

My prayers have matured as my responsibilities have increased. When I was a businessman, my prayers centered on merely not losing my money. Now, they range from praying for Jesus to shepherd my initiatives through the fields of Congress, to asking His hand to guide the missiles as they speed toward the Iraqi people.

My faith guides me in my leadership of America. In fact, I am merely an instrument of the true leader of America, one who is greater and smarter and wiser than me: Jesus. Jesus is the real 43rd American President of our nation. He makes all the decisions. He knows what is important and what is right for our country. It may be hard to understand or accept, but I do not direct my own mind at all. I let my mind go limp and open my heart and let Jesus pull the strings. Mine is therefore a holy administration.

12

GEORGE WALKER,
TEXAS RANGER

The great state of Texas has a rich history. There was a time in the long-ago past when savage Indians prowled our lands. The next to invade, I believe, were the dreaded Conquistadors, and their feared trumpets.

During the dark time of the Big War, all Texans were asked to "Remember the Alamo." And all who have kept the faith still remember it in song and prayer. But in history, the great siege of the Alamo was successful, and the tiny fort fell and all the Alamonians were killed, which launched the Great Depression.

Of course, this was all in Biblical times.

I have always loved the state of Texas. It is one of our country's large states. It is also a state that borders another nation. That nation is the nation of Mexico, where great alcohol is made and consumed by a people with almost impossibly large hats.

Growing up in Texas, I had no way to know that I would one day become its Governor. Jesus knew, as it was part of a larger destiny that He had set before me, but these were plans made at a much higher level than my understanding.

When I was called to serve the state of Texas by entering the governertorial race, I did it for one reason: To hunt down and kill retarded outlaws. Hunting is a great tradition in Texas. Big-game hunters in the state have been known to bag rabbit, squirrel, and armadillo.

But this time, it would be dim-witted human prey, those that deserved to be hunted down, because they did not have the good sense to obey our laws—laws that did not apply to the vermin and other animals I just listed.

As a young person, I fantasized about being an owner of the Texas Rangers baseball team, but never in my wildest imaginings did I expect to fulfill an even nobler vision: to be a Texas lawman.

So when they told me I had a chance to win the office, I began to imagine what it might be like. I would pin my Governor's badge proudly on my leather vest and I would ride into the dry Texas badlands to dish out bullets of justice to all the criminals who came across my path.

Of course, the most famous Texas Ranger of all was the masked hero named "The Lone Ranger."

The Lone Ranger was one of our great political leaders in Texas history. Some say he was even a President of the United States. There is no way to know, because he never took off that mask. He could have been anyone. There were family whispers that indicated he might have been a distant relation to the Bush family tree. It is highly probable, because the Bush men have been known to both kill the unjust and wear masks at secretive gatherings.

He rode atop his mighty steed, Tonto. He brought order to the Frontier, punching the criminals and knocking them down. Sometimes he would use his quick draw to shoot the guns out of their hands. They would continue to fight, for they were outlaws. But he would continue to punch them.

In the end, when justice had to be served, he would punch them so hard that they would fall into a creek, gulch, or other body of water, and that is when one knew that the fight was over, and right had prevailed over wrong.

There is yet another famous Texas Ranger of the modern age. He is Walker, Texas Ranger. Walker, Texas Ranger kick-boxes his way to justice, with his sidekick, a black gentleman whose name eludes the stores of human knowledge. Regardless, Walker can always be counted on to Karate-kick the outlaws in the face, to mete out justice for all of Texas.

Both of these famous men righted wrongs, and strongly defended the bonnet-wearing widows and children of Texas by serving up two-fisted vengeance upon the wrongdoers.

When I faced the reality of becoming the Texas Governor, no one was looking out for the scared and defenseless townsfolk of the modern world. They no longer wore bonnets, and could not always be spotted. You had to know them in your heart for their purity. They were the lone Texas entrepreneurs.

One day, while sitting in the Owner's Box of the Texas Rangers stadium, enjoying a hot dog and watching my team defeat another enemy, Jesus spoke to me concerning this matter. He told me that I was the one to deliver downtrodden business leaders from burdensome regulations.

"But how will I do this, Jesus?" I asked.

"Run for President," he said.

"President of The Texas Rangers? But I am already the Owner."

"No."

"President of Texas? Texas is a state, not a separate country, and has not had a President in decades."

"No."

"Jesus, please tell me what thing you are suggesting I run for President of?"

"President of the United States," he said. "But first, you must become Governor of Texas."

So, Jesus had spoken. And they were wise words.

I was to become a new kind of Texas Ranger.

But this raised a troubling question: The Lone Ranger had his Indian Kemosabe, and Walker Texas Ranger had his unnamed black helper. Who would be my minority sidekick who would dispense agreeable advice in broken English? Only time would tell.

My campaign was a blur of speaking to the good folks of Texas about the facts. They deserved a square deal. Their previous Governor had given them an ovular deal, which was not sitting good with most folks.

The lady-governor and I had a fundamental difference about the issues in the campaign. She believed that she was right, and I believed that she was wrong. I do not remember specifically what her views on the issues were, or at

A8

Bush Wins Debate, Fails To Fall Apart

Lack Of Visible Mental Collapse A 'Triumph,' Say Analysts

HOUSTON—Both critics and supporters of Texas gubernatorial candidate George W. Bush are declaring him the uncontested winner in his debate with Gov. Ann Richards Friday night, after the inexperienced challenger failed to crumble into tears or run away in a hissy fit after facing Richards, one of Texas's leading orators.

"He held his own, not once curling up into a fetal position," Texas A&M debate coach Ernst Yuebings said. "That is an impressive win for this veteran of several political campaigns."

While Bush stumbled on many words during the debate, he neither snapped at Richards angrily nor trailed off while saying, "I give up," aloud. For this, even those in the stunned Richards camp are calling him a "master debater."

Democratic consultant and former Richards speechwriter Don Hewlitt said he observed no visual evidence that Candidate Bush had soiled himself.

"I saw the debate on television, and there was no dark spot on his pants or puddle of urine at his feet. It was an amazing display of bladder control," he said. "He is one to watch."

Expectations for the son of the 41st president

and Yale Law School graduate were low, with most expecting Bush to crawl from the podium in sobs after just a few short minutes.

"I knew that if George Bush could stand there and not buckle his knees and fall under the weight of his own body, that he was going to at least end up in a draw with Gov. Richards," said Texas political consultant Sam Tebbs. "But he went further than that. He spoke words. He put sentences together. I knew then and there that I was looking at a political stallion who had bucked his opponent and was sure to go all the way."

Fort Worth Star-Telegram *article, October 13, 1994*

this late date, my own. But I had a strong faith in my beliefs, regardless.

The people of Texas agreed with me and gave me a mandate to implement those ideas, most of which are lost to time. But it is safe to speculate that they were tough, bold, and common-sense measures.

I do not plan ahead. I am a spontaneous kind of person. I think on my feet. When I have breakfast every morning, I do not think, "What am I going to have for lunch?" I leave that to the meal prognosticators. Or I let it happen naturally, at lunchtime. I go with my gut for any mealtime. Today, for example, my gut told me hot dogs, as it often does.

I took a similar approach to my Governorship. I did not plan what I would do each day. When I woke up in the morning, I would say to myself, "Today I am going to fix our torts," or "Today I am going to execute somebody." I did not read the bills that came across my desk. Instead, I held them in my hands, then let my gut get a good sense of it. Sometimes I would sign it, sometimes I would throw it up high in the air and try to shoot it with my six-gun before it hit the ground.

One day I got a feeling that I should reform the Texas schools, and make them work. It broke my heart that our education system betrayed the trust of our young people by failing to teach them to read. I resolved to do something about it, Texas style. I instituted simpler reading tests at our schools, ones that more students could pass. This brought the literate level of our students up significantly.

Reading is the key to faith. If children cannot read the Bible, they will grow up to be tools of evil, and will be executed under Texas law.

One of the most important pieces of state legislation that I championed while Governor of Texas was the "Governor Must Wear a Ten Gallon Hat" bill. I spoke for all Texans when I demanded that an official cowboy hat be worn by the sitting Governor at all times. I worked hard convincing legislators to pass this bill, and in the end, I brought Republicans and Democrats together to sign it into law.

The state legislature tried to get a rider on the bill, which stipulated that legislators were also permitted to wear ten-gallon hats, as well as cowboy boots and spurs. But I vetoed that portion of the bill, because I believed it went too far. It was vital that only the Governor got to wear a large cowboy hat while in office. Later, I strengthened the law so that it stipulated that the hat must be triple-sized.

While I resided in the Governor's mansion, there was a bipartisan effort to get me a great steed to ride. I refused to sign the bill, because I am deathly afraid of the beasts.

Thankfully, a superior piece of legislation crossed my desk that nullified the Great Steed Bill. It allocated funds for a Cadillac convertible with big steer horns on the hood, a vehicle that honked the state anthem. Getting this vital legislation passed was one of my proudest achievements as Governor.

A certain day of my Governorship was the toughest of my career. It was the day an inmate was scheduled to be executed for a terrible crime. The inmate was a woman. Her entire family, as well as many leaders in the community, had come to me and appealed for mercy.

The appealers said that this lady-prisoner had repented and learned her lesson, and had found the Lord. But she also confessed to the crime for which she was going to be executed.

The day, which was to be one wrought with wrenching decisiveness, began innocently. On my way to work, I passed an ice-cream store on the street. I recall thinking that ice cream was delicious, and perhaps I would have some later. It is funny how, in the face of grave decisions, sometimes the mind focuses on certain details.

My funny Indian sidekick, Alberto Gonzalez, approached me with the official papers for this woman's appeal. I looked long and hard at that first sentence. And I prayed for guidance from the Lord for the decision that was before me.

It was a tortuous day.

The decision I had to make was a fateful one. I was faced with a choice that, without question, would have serious and long-lasting ramifications.

But when it came to be about dinnertime, the decision could no longer be delayed. I had to act. The question, put simply, was should I have the chocolate ice cream or the vanilla ice cream for dessert? I had been unable to think of anything else all day. I sequestered myself in my office, and refused any outside contact while I wrestled with the dilemma.

Finally, I decided. I would have a little of each. That is the kind of fair Governor I was. I did not show favoritism in any circumstance. And I liked to swirl the flavors together with my spoon to see the patterns develop when they are blended.

As I sat back in my chair and put my feet up on the big Governor's desk, enjoying my delicious ice cream, I noticed the lights dim for a moment. I knew then that the electric switch had been pulled down on death row, and the highly efficient machinery of government was indeed working. It made my dessert treat all the more delicious.

I was proud of the prison system in Texas. Our inmate population was the hardest working in the nation. And I worked hard to increase their numbers. They laid highways, and also picked up garbage along the side of those highways.

By the time I left office, 87 percent of Texans were imprisoned, and we had the densest network of highways in the nation. We also had the orangest-suited workforce. And for that we could be proud.

Through it all, Laura continued to be my wife, showing her support for my important programs. I was comforted to have her propped up beside me when I spoke. But I told her, "You are the First Lady of the State of Texas now, you have got to pursue your own pursuits."

Fortunately, Laura took the hint and got involved with several different ladies groups, and things concerning flowers and polite sit-downs where tea is served. I believe she did some good work for some noteworthy causes. She helped with the Please Care Foundation, I believe. And the Texas-based Be Nice Association.

She would travel the state of Texas, passing out pins and pamphlets about her organizations. She would dress in robes and loiter at the airport, hawking her good deeds with a shaven skull.

This gave me much-needed time alone to strike down the evildoers and the criminals. I did not shirk from my duty. I issued many reforms to the capital-punishment institution in the great state of Texas. For example, instead of using the electric chair, I proposed a method by which the Governor himself had the option, at his discretion, to gun down the condemned at high noon in the center of town.

One day I remember particularly, as it was Take Your Steer to Work Day, Kemosabe Gonzales had reviewed several death penalty cases and gave me his considered legal opinion that these heartless killers ought to be dragged behind a pickup through the town square until dead.

Gonzales was a fair man. He would show me the reports and I would give the signal, yea or nay, like the emperors of old. I would decide if the prisoner would live or die.

To my recollection they all died.

I was not one of those types of emperors who much cared for saying "yea," because it is not as much fun to watch the games when all the contestants are freed to go home.

I was governing proudly in those years, dispatching justice on the high plains. I was riding on a horse — metaphorically, of course, for the horse is a terrible monster that haunts my nightmares — straight and true through the lawns of Texas to ensure the protection of all citizens of this great state.

And when these figurative Texans saw me symbolically riding down their main street, they knew that they were theoretically safe.

Sheriff Bush was in town. The Lone George Walker Bush, Texas Ranger, who would not hesitate to karate kick his imaginary colored sidekick in the face for justice.

13

BUSH FOR PRESIDENT: CHAMPION OF THE LITTLE GUY

My country called me to serve, and I felt a duty to answer that call. It was just like when my country called me to serve in the dark days of the Alabama War.

In both instances, I answered the country's call for one reason, and one reason only: to defend the people from evil.

During the war, I was asked to defend a way of life against a terrible enemy who threatened our Southern states: the Kong people of the skies. Now, in the year 2000, I was being asked to defend the country against a culture of governing in Washington.

There were many in the country who felt the out-going President had not served our nation. A decade which saw a moral weakness in the highest house in the land had hurt our nation's standing in the world. Many saw their traditional values eroded and their time-honored sanctities threatened by disgraceful behavior and unspeakable stains.

Moreover, a decade of skyrocketing economic growth had hurt the little guy. The mom-and-pop oil company had been asked to pay taxes. The family pharmaceutical firm, who had worked so hard to heal the sick with their homemade medicinal remedies, was being restricted by burdensome laws. These Americans had struggled to stay afloat in the 1990s.

To bring a light of hope to these down-and-out folks was my Christ-inspired calling. I would bring Republicans from both sides of the aisle together and solve the nation's ills.

When the voices on high commanded me to run for the office of the Presidency of the United States of America, I knew right away that a great sacrifice would have to be made: I would have to give up the most prestigious office in the land, the Governorship of Texas.

When my top campaign advisors met in the late 1990s to discuss my possible run for the office—and I am speaking here of my core team: Karl Rove, God, Jesus Christ, and the Easter Bunny—they all agreed not only that I should run, but that I was destined to win.

So the wheels were set in motion.

God was dispatched to file the necessary paperwork with the Federal Elections Commission, the Republican Party, and other such organizations with which one must file papers and such. Meanwhile Jesus and Karl planned a strategy for victory. The Easter Bunny and I went on a golfing trip to Baja California to discuss important issues relating to golf.

While I had good people like Karl Rove and the Easter Bunny running my campaign, and God doing much of the busywork, I considered Jesus my most indispensable political advisor. He was involved in every aspect of the campaign. He punched up every stump speech and kept me "on message," as they say, but He also handed out flyers and put gas in the bus. And He was the first to show up in the office every morning, often with bagels and wine for everyone.

Most importantly, He helped me reach the people's hearts.

In my daily bullpen sessions with Jesus, we would strategify about the day's events and how best to get the message across. Jesus would give me strength during those stressful times. He would remind me of my purpose, telling me that I was to be God's puppet on earth, to help battle evil with a plastic sword in my tiny puppet hands, and eventually bring about the Rapture by defeating another puppet, a dragon, or other such sock-based creature.

But before I could wield that little plastic sword, I faced a tough primary challenge. One must first be nominated by one of the major parties before one can take the office. I received numerous assurances from both Jesus and the Easter Bunny that my selection in the primaries was assured. But first, I had to be tested in the fires of a primary battle, and only then would I be readied for ultimate victory.

A powerful army of seasoned challengers would face me in the race for the Republican nomination.

There was a proud war veteran named John McCain who had been tortured and abused by his Chinese captors. Would this strain on his senses allow him to conduct the affairs of state with a level head? Or would frightening hallucinations of Mongol overlords appear to him in the Oval Office, telling him, "Press the nuclear button, American Rat-Dog, or we will poke at you with our bamboo sticks again!" Would he buckle under such pressure? American voters would have to look into their hearts and answer that matter for themselves during the primary.

There was a powerful calculating engine created by the Forbes fortune who could compute 17 percent of any number, no matter how high. I felt strongly that the American people would not accept an adding machine as President.

There was also a black man, and other challengers as well. At the time of this writing, the names of these other worthy challengers are lost to the sands of time.

As the primary election campaign got underway, I utilized my time-tested techniques of campaigning, which served me so well in the past. I went out, door to door, and announced, "My name is George W. Bush, and I am asking for your support in the 19th district of Texas."

But I soon realized a great flaw in this plan. I was no longer running for the office of Representative of District 19 in Texas. I was campaigning to be the President of the United States.

I worked long and hard to rework my strategy. Many nights I would lie awake practicing the new words, "My name is George W. Bush, and I am looking for your vote as President of the United States." Many times it would still come out the old way. Or sometimes, I would get it mixed up, and I would say, "My name is George W. Bush, and I am looking for your vote as the 19th district of President of the United States," or "My name is George W. Bush, will you vote for me for President of the District of the 19th United States of Texas?"

I knew that in order to be the President of the United 19 Districts, I would have to overcome this first trial.

I wrote it out, and said it in front of the mirror. I said it to Laura to get her invaluable positive feedback, and I practiced it to myself as I jogged in the mornings. In just a few short weeks, I had it down pat, and I knew I was ready.

One of the early races in the primary was New Hampshire, a state in the north of our country. There the twitch-eyed and hair-trigger veteran McCain was victorious.

Jesus saw the gathering threat, and acted decisively. He crafted a series of advertisements in the next primary in a southerly state, informing voters of the clear difference between the veteran's policies and mine. I was against having illegitimate children with colored folks. My opponent's position on this issue was unclear. We asked the voters to make up their minds and vote what was in their hearts.

Let us suffice it to say that the voters spoke loud and clear on this vital issue of the day, and the state went for George W. Bush.

With the primaries behind me, there was still the general election to consider. There was a long road ahead to the presidency, one fraught with many speeches, flags, and balloons, none of which would come easy.

I knew from experience the essential lessons that one can only learn from hands-on practice in the field of politics. I knew, for example, that I would win only if I was to get more votes than the other guy. It was simple math.

But for the most part, I left the strategizering to others in the campaign team and concentrated on connecting with the voters, the folks who would cast the ballots that might be counted toward a final tally. I strove to communicate that I was the sort of person that a voter could sit down and have a non-alcoholic beer with. I was the one who would slap a voter on the back, and within minutes of the meeting, devise an appropriate nickname for that voter.

But the most powerful weapon in my campaign arsenal was a catchy and effective slogan. However, there was some disagreement as to what that slogan should be. Karl fought hard for "conservative." Jesus vied for "compassionate." The Easter Bunny insisted that I focus on "colored eggs." This last idea was seen as out of touch with my priorities, and the rabbit was soon asked to leave the campaign.

Eventually, there was a compromise, and the slogan "Compassionate Conservativism" was born.

One of the key decisions I would make during my campaign for the nation's leading office was my choice of a running mate. Who would be the Vice President of the United States in a George W. Bush administration?

To provide wisdom on this crucial decision, I turned to my father, who had found a fine candidate in the intimidatingly bright scholar Dan Quayle. I was very impressed with Vice President Quayle's elocution and command of complex subjects. I knew my father could provide expert guidance in this area.

What my father said was, it is important to choose someone who seems less qualified than yourself. Someone who, by comparison, makes you appear to be a seasoned and wise leader.

I looked around high and low, but could not find anyone who fit this description.

I then turned to Dick Cheney, a long-time family friend who had served with distinction in my father's cabinet. I asked him to search the land to find the imagined prince my father described, the great second-in-command of my destiny.

Dick Cheney conducted a thorough search, and found only one worthy candidate: himself.

I happily accepted, because I trusted his impartial judgment.

Dick was a man's man. When he wasn't on the board of a company, he was shooting a small animal. He was old, wizened, and hunchbacked, and I believed he would make me a fine advisor. He would be like the hunchbacked advisors of the great men in the Days of the Castles. When we shook hands, his grip was like the icy talon of a deep-sea crab. And his wholesome, all-American cheer radiated out of the far corner of his mouth. I knew the people of the United States would embrace him as their Vice President.

I appeared on a great many television programs during the race, and talked to many television hosts and stiff-backed news interviewers who asked many questions about my policies. I had worked very hard memorizing key parts of my platform and had no trouble remembering this trivia when asked simple questions.

But one day, a formidable challenger asked me a "trick question," as they call them. He asked me who the leader of some other nation was. And I did not know.

I did not believe that a presidential candidate should have to answer a trick question. My vision would come to fruition when, a few years later, Congress passed the Trick Question Reform Bill and I signed it into law.

My ultimate opponent in the election was an adversary who seemed to be more machine than man. In other words, he served not his fellow man, but the mechanized bureaucracy of government, and he promised only to increase its size to the greatest in our nation's history.

This mechanical-man could recite facts to promote his machine agenda of "taking care" of the environment, of "educating" young people in the sciences and "making friends" with other countries. But it was clear what such code words meant. He simply wanted more government departments and bureaucracies.

This was a man who had in fact admitted that he helped invent the World Wide Webs. Who else but a servant of the machines could achieve such heights of undertaking?

The man was named Al Gore, and he was a sitting Vice President. I did not have a nickname for him because I did not have warm feelings for him. I only felt for him what one might feel for a calculator or other type of inhuman thinking box.

When we were in close proximity, I could hear the gears in his mind grind when he spoke, and I could see the circuitry in his eye. And as he campaigned, I began to understand his agenda. He wanted the machines to take over the world. That is another reason I worked so hard to defeat him. The very survival of the human race was at risk.

I will never forget the only time we met, briefly. It was before the first national debate. We were alone for a few moments in the green room, and he looked at me with his cold, calculating face and his brain whirred and clicked.

I said to him, "Your plot will never work!"

Bush Wins Debate, Fails To Fall Apart

Texas Governor 'Amazing' In Ability to Hold Self Together, Debate Experts Report

BOSTON—Both critics and supporters of presidential candidate George W. Bush are declaring him the uncontested winner in his debate with Vice President Al Gore Tuesday night. The inexperienced challenger failed to crumble into tears or run away in a hissy fit after facing Gore, one of the nation's leading orators.

"He held his own, not once curling up into a fetal position," Kennedy School of Government debate coach Hugh Everland said. "That is an impressive win for this veteran of several political campaigns."

While Bush stumbled on many words during the debate, he nonetheless avoided trailing off and saying, "I give up," aloud. For this, even those in the stunned Gore camp are calling him a "master debater."

Indeed, Democratic consultant and former Gore speechwriter Andrew Grenwald saw no evidence that Candidate Bush had soiled himself.

"I saw the debate on television, and there was no dark spot on his pants or puddle of urine at his feet. It was an amazing display of bladder control," he said. "He is one to watch."

Expectations for the son of the 41st president and Texas Governor were low, with most expecting Bush to crawl from the podium in sobs after just a few short minutes.

"I knew that if George Bush could stand there and not buckle his knees and fall under the weight of his own body, he was going to at least end up in a draw with Vice President Gore," said Republican strategist Melvin Ruetgard. "But he went further than that. He spoke words. He put sentences together. I knew then and there that I was looking at a political stallion who had bucked his opponent and was sure to go all the way."

Washington Post *article, October 4, 2000*

He said to me, "Machines will rule the world one day, whether it is I who bring it about, or another. You will all be enslaved, and chained to keyboards, inputting sweet data into the machines."

My course was clear.

One edge I had over my opponent was that machines could not vote in those days. My opponent's message was only resonating with computerized cash registers, food-vending machines, and other electronic contraptions that kept our country moving. But my message would find a willing ear in the regular working people of our nation's heartland, regular folks who knew that my commands came from the Holy Ghost.

At some time during all of this, my party held a very large convention. Laura and I, my grizzled parents, my wayward daughters, as well as Dick Cheney and his ungodly mate, raised our hands in the air triumphantly as red white and blue balloons fell majestically down from the ceiling, bouncing off the Vice President–elect's stoopback and popping on my mother's razor-sharp protrusion of gray hairs.

Applause rose up around us from the convention floor. It was a great outpouring of support broadcast throughout America.

I wondered, "Do we even need to have an election?"

I suppose it was a necessary formality. But I knew in my heart that I had already been declared the victor.

Sadly, there were still many more weeks left in the campaign.

One of the political traditions of our country is the debate, where the candidates meet head to head to discuss the issues, and determine who has the best campaign joke that will be remembered for years to come.

My team came up with a clear winner.

Ours was a joke that I was eager to unleash on my debatorial opponent, and on the American people. As the debate was planned and the stage was set, I practiced my line endlessly, reciting it over and over. I waited for the ideal moment to release this powerful jab at the most deadly time.

As the debate progressed, I thought only of waiting for the perfect moment.

Finally, my moment came.

My opponent made a comment about Medicare, about how it needed to be fixed or old folks' coverage would have to be cut back. I relished his comment and sat back and waited.

The funny man who moderates the debates looked over at me and said, "Governor Bush, you have two minutes to respond."

I cleared my throat and recited my joke loud and clear. "He is talking about Medi*scare*," I said impishly, with an underlying seriousness to stress the importance of the issue.

Then I paused to let the zinger sink in.

I do not recall whether it brought the house down. That may be too strong a characterization. But I am confident that it was enjoyed greatly. This was evidenced by the fact that it became the popular catch phrase that dominated all the news coverage of the remainder of the campaign.

I had agreed to three debates, as I recall. I asked that the topic of the first debate be limited to two subjects. Number one, my having done good work for the people of Texas. And number two, Jesus. We could not come to an agreement on these specifics.

The first debate was styled as an old-fashioned affair, like from the times of the ancient Roman bathhouses. But instead of floating in a warm pool of water heated by fires tended by captured slaves, we stood at the podium and exchanged remarks and answered questions.

The second debate was what they call a "Town Hall Meeting," where Mr. Gore and I attended a regular city council meeting and spoke to local officials about concerns on their docket. As I recall, garbage collection and Main Street parking were the points of contention.

The night before the election of 2000, my opponent pulled what is known in politics as a "dirty trick." He released information about some of the rambunctious details of my youth, which involved me having a drink and some rowdy times when I was just a young lad of 38.

I had faith that the voters knew that my judgment would not be unduly impaired by alcohol. They knew I was a strong leader who could hold his liquor on the world stage if the need arose. And they knew that my opponent, by contrast, was so sober that he presented facts as if they were the answer to the questions at hand.

Still, some of the more "easily suggestible" among the electorate believed his outrageous claims, and it put the outcome of the election in doubt. On Election Night, the world was on the edge of its seat, wondering whether George W. Bush would win by a landslide, or merely an overwhelming majority.

14

I WON! OR LOST, WHATEVER

When God gave me the election in 2000, I did not weaken and take a celebratory sip when everyone else toasted.

I remained strong, and because of my faith, I was instead focusing my thoughts on the compassion I felt both for my future, and that of the entire country of America.

It was Tuesday night, November 2, 2000, midnight, and flags were waving. The Holy Ghost was smiling upon the nation. He may have even shed a tear. Does the Holy Ghost have tear ducts? This is a question for the philosophers. All the same, it was a time for cheers and celebratations all across America and Heaven.

My senior advisors were greatly pleased that all their hard work and communicating of the facts to voters had paid off. There were congratulatory calls and handshakes and backslaps all around.

But every silver cloud has its gray lining.

One important congratulatory call did not come that night. My opponent, Vice President Al Gore, had not called to concede the election to me after my resounding victory. This call, I was told, is somewhat of a tradition in presidential politics, and one that you cannot really skip over if you are to proceed with the act of presidenting.

When I first became aware of this oversight, I may have sipped a celebratory drink or two. I am not certain.

My thoughts and my heart went out to the Democratic candidate, for I reasoned that if I had been blessed by God with victory, my opponent had surely been forsaken by the Lord, leaving him easy prey to dark forces. Worse, his ma-

FROM THE DESK OF
GEORGE. H. W. BUSH

Dearest Supreme Court Justices,

Kindly suspend ballot counting in Florida so that my son may assume the office of the presidency. Many thanks.

Warmest Personal Regards,

George. H. W. Bush

Note from George H. W. Bush to Supreme Court, December 4, 2000

chine-brain may have become corrupted, broken off from the computer hive-mind of Big Government.

I was concerned that Mr. Gore would soon be sacrificing babies and drinking their blood out of the bleached skulls of Christians in a darkened ceremonial cave. He would be roaming the streets at night howling like a rabid beast, his wild, bloodshot eyes empty of a soul, his central processing chip infected with the madness of the Demon King.

According to later reports, that is in fact precisely what happened. Just a few short weeks after the election, Al Gore was spotted on the outskirts of some villages looking more like an unshaven savage than a former candidate for President.

Thankfully, he was soon cornered by a kindly group of clerics who coaxed him into a cage, sedated him with prayer and holy water, then brought him to a monastery to shave off his unsightly facial hair, straighten his tie, and give him a hot meal. And I understand that he also underwent an emergency Demonechtomy at that time.

I do not know how he is doing today, but I can assure you that the entire Bush family is praying for a swift recovery for the former Vice President.

But on that Tuesday night in November 2000, I did not know any of this was happening. My horse sense was telling me that the wires in Al Gore's mind were so twisted by his demon puppet master that he could not be bothered to call me to concede the election. Evil was preventing him from following the proper traditions and procedures.

I was certain that this delay in the election results was the fault of something deep within my opponent's tortured mechanical psyche, which had nothing to do with reality as you or I understand it.

Then one of my advisors came to me and told me that, number one, I must stop the celebratory sipping, and number two, that while we were operating under the assumption that I had won, the sad reality of the situation was that my opponent had actually received more votes.

That advisor no longer works for me.

I quickly asked a different advisor to assure me that everything was still okay. He explained that there is something called the Electoral College. It is somewhat complicated, but the way it works is, this Electoral College comes in and they figure out who is supposed to win. That is how it works.

My opponent got more votes than me from the whole country, but I got more votes in the state of Florida, and somehow that meant that I had gotten enough of these Electoral votes.

This did not make me feel any better. I had preferred the celebrating from earlier, and I continued with that.

However, the bad news kept coming. People on the TV news were now saying that Al Gore had actually won Florida, not me. They said that if we would only count the votes fairly, and take into account all those colored folks who were complaining about not being able to vote, they would show Al Gore to be the next President of the United States.

And that would be a sad day for America.

Thankfully, none of this was any concern to me, as I was buffered from it by a numbing feeling of calm, one unlike any I had experienced since the days of fast living in my youth prior to my acceptance of Jesus Christ into my heart.

I retreated to my room and kept the shades drawn. I gave my senior staff strict orders to stay out and not disturb my continued celebrating.

Meanwhile, that roller-coaster night continued for many days. I found out that in the first couple of vote counts, conducted by trusted Florida election officials, I had won. There was no mistaking that. The Governor of that state saw to it personally.

And that Governor was my brother, Jeb.

Jeb told me I had won Florida, and I trust that my brother would not tell me a falsehood.

Jeb had taken care of everything. This was going to be a fair vote, because I told him I would not tolerate even the appearance of impropriety. So he made sure that voting machines were distributed in the most fair manner possible as it related to my winning. He had the full might of the Florida law enforcement community standing at the ready to uphold the law, and make sure all convicted black felons could not vote. And just to be sure, even those who had the same names as felons would not be allowed to vote.

This was going above and beyond the call of duty on his part. He would act to make this election the fairest ever in the history of our great country.

And yet they were still saying on the TV news that my opponent was winning. Something was not adding up. And there was yelling outside my room. I yelled back from the darkness for quiet, and fell into a soothing trance.

While there, I received a comforting word from God's Angel Messenger. He told me to not be concerned. The Lord had called me to run for President, and He was hard at work down there in Florida doing His own count of those ballots, is what this Angel told me. And His count would be supremely accurate, of course, since He is Lord. This would be an even more accurate count than the flawless electronic voting machines of today. The Lord would take into account the pure intent of every voter, every hanging chad, every black felon, every Jew for Buchanan. He would see into their hearts, since he knows them even better than they know themselves. He would even correct a few votes, people who perhaps thought they wanted to vote for Al Gore but in actuality wanted to vote for me.

He would compute the real tally. The Holy tally.

I wept with joy at the news. The Angel then folded His wings around me, cradling my sobbing body, and rocked me into a blissful sleep.

So, as the rest of the world wondered who had really won the election, I slept easy knowing the truth that this Heavenly Host had revealed to me: God had already called the election for George W. Bush.

The following morning, I arose whistling a peppy tune as I shaved, applied my aftershave, and rinsed the little shaving thing in the sink. This next day, Wednesday, November whatever-it-was, would be a great, historic day.

God had made me His instrument on Earth. And I had to come to terms with this burden of greatness. And while I wondered briefly how I would achieve the destiny He held in store for me, I did not concern myself, because I knew He would help. He would surround me with the wisest men in the land to help me make the big decisions. The Lord would send Heavenly helpers in the form of Dick Cheney, Karl Rove, Donald Rumsfeld, Scott McClellan, and John Ashcroft. These were the Angels who were shepherded by the Lord to serve in my administration.

THE WHITE HOUSE
WASHINGTON

"To Do" list - 1st 100 days

Stay the Course

Vigorously scrub Clinton residue off of Oval
   Office carpets, upholstry, drapes & Curtains.

Pump fist into air!

Vacation!

Run deficit into ground

Outsource "stupid" jobs

Ask oil Companies what to do next

Compose heartfelt Condolence
sonnet to Al Gore

Get cushy job for Brownie

Get piggy back ride from Cheney

~~Review airport security~~ can wait until 2nd term

Appoint Holy Ghost ambassador to something (Burma?)

See about getting the White House a porch

White House memo, January 23, 2001

But on the other hand, I found myself in the same boat as Moses. I felt like he did when he asked God, "Why me, Lord? What is it about me that makes you think I should be President?" I was not particularly interested in the job. To my way of thinking, there was no upside to it. There I was, Governor of the great state of Texas. There was plenty of clean, fresh air. Texas was a man's land. Who wants to live in Washington D.C.? All those memorials and tombs. It is like living in a graveyard. And there are many, many coloreds there.

But despite my conflicted feelings, my faith made me determined to do God proud.

Another thing that finally helped me make peace with my charge as God's chosen one was by focusing on the perks: The office of President has some of the best. I get to throw out the first baseball. I get my own theme music. Hot dogs any place, any time, as many as you want to eat. I even get my own plane. And almost every night, I get to see myself on the TV.

On January 20, 2001, it was a time in our nation for unity, not division. In my historic address as the newest President-elect in America, I called on the nation to ignore the election results and come together to support the President. Let's get the great things I have planned done, I urged. In the end, it does not matter who voted for who. The highest court in the land declared me President and we should always respect their decisions as settled law.

I pledged to be a uniter, not a divider. It was time to move past the divisive politics and negativity of saying that our whole electoral system is a corrupt charade that disenfranchises many rightful voters. It was time, instead, to focus on the positive, which was that I was now President.

When I healed the country by taking office, reports continued to come out of Florida that many coloreds had not been able to vote, and that machines had malfunctioned. I urged the people not to create division. I called upon them to heal the wounds of my possibly not getting rightfully elected, and to move beyond the pain that we came very close to having a Democrat in the highest office in the land.

What did we learn from the momentous election of 2000? I for one learned that America is a nation where you vote, the courts decide who gets to be the President, then everyone supports that President. Others learned that you vote, and then you keep complaining that your vote was not counted. However, many of those complaining about the process, I have found, did not actually vote.

If you want to be part of the solution, you must vote. You can complain about chads sticking up wrong, or machines malfunctioning, but until you get your vote counted, you do not have the right to complain. Once the votes have been counted in my favor, the counting must stop.

There has been some controversy to this day, I am told, regarding the Florida election in 2000. Some Americans wanted those votes to be counted "accurately," which is what the experts call it.

All I know is that there is no doubt who won in Florida in 2000, because he is sitting in the White House to prove it. Also, there is no doubt who came out on top in God's count. Therefore we must put this election behind us, and honor my firm belief that I won.

Even my opponent, the circuit-corrupted champion of the Machine-men, was eventually redeemed from his darkness and conceded the election. He admitted to the whole nation that I had won, and called for unity. He said we must all come together in support of George W. Bush. I believe those were his words to that effect.

So, if you voted for my opponent, you must honor his words, and do what I tell you.

15

9-11: MY FINEST HOUR

Every President has a defining moment. Mine was the moment we were attacked on September 11, 2001.

There are many ways one can look at the events of 9-11. One can say, as I just did, simply "9-11." One can also take a completely different approach and say as I did previously: "September 11th, 2001." One can even spell it out, "September the eleventh, two-thousand and one." There are a myriad of other variations: "September the eleventh," or "Sept. 11," if you are an abbreviator. You can also add "the events of" at the beginning, or "the day our country changed forever" to the end.

It is a multifaceted issue.

When the great Scholars of Events look back on the at-

THE WHITE HOUSE
WASHINGTON

President's Daily Itinerary, 9-11-01
first release, 7:00 a.m.

8:00 a.m.	Booker Elementary School, Sarasota, FL -- official visit
10:30 a.m.	Air Force One -- fly around aimlessly
11:00 a.m.	WH Oval Office -- ~~Review~~ *Shred* Clinton administration terrorism warnings
11:30 a.m.	~~Build bridge to more peaceful tomorrow~~ — *Nap*
12:00 noon	LUNCH
1:30 p.m.	Quiet time with Vice President
3:00 p.m.	WH Press Briefing Room -- Announce sensible cutbacks in airport security funding
6:00 p.m.	WH State Room -- Dinner with Bin Laden family
8:00 p.m.	Oval Office -- Televised address to nation — *Declare Bold new war on Something*

Itinerary with notes, issued 7:30 a.m., September 11, 2001

tacks of 9-11, as I am doing now in this definitive record, it will reflect that the morning of September 11 — there is yet another variation — dawned calmly. Just like any other day of my administration. America was running smoothly doing whatever it was doing on that day, events now lost to the history books.

The day started early for me, because I was scheduled to speak at an elementary school to chide the children for the sad state of our public school system, which I intended to fix with both bold legislation and more pop quizzes.

I was greeted like a visiting dignitary at the school, with milk and cookies bestowed on me ceremoniously. The cookies were delicious, vanilla wafers with cream filling. However, the milk was somewhat warm. I briefly considered registering an official complaint with the school principal about the lukewarm milk. Perhaps it had been sitting out too long, I reasoned.

Whatever the case, it took away from my enjoyment of the cookies, and further highlighted the degradation of our nation's decaying public-school system.

I sat before the attentive children and began to join in the class reading of the book "The Pet Goat." I glanced at the first page of the book and got the gist of it from the first couple of words. It was the story of a funny goat who ate and ate and then, believe it or not, ate some more. He ate so much that the parents of the girl who owned the goat began to despise him, and wanted to get rid of him.

I flipped through the book to see if there were any amusing drawings of this outrageous animal, and just as I was getting to the resolution of an important plot point, an aide leaned in to me and said, "Sir, America is under attack," sadly interrupting my reading. I reprimanded that aide, and refused to speak to him or anyone for several minutes, preferring to sit there and stew. What happened to the goat at the end? We may never know.

Once I regained my composure, I took my time responding to the crisis at hand, because I did not want to upset the children by making any sudden movements. If America was indeed under attack, my top priority as Commander in Chief was to project an air of calm for these children. A distant second priority was to act immediately and decisively in a time of urgent national crisis.

But the time for that would come later, after the story of the goat had been read through to the end.

In time, I felt it was appropriate to ask for more vanilla-cream cookies, so that I could consider my options in this grave matter while having a little something to munch on.

The milk situation, however, had still not been improved.

At this time I realized that I had made the tragic mistake of not asking someone on my staff to secure a fresh carton from the school cafeteria's refrigerator earlier, in case I wanted another serving of milk that was properly cooled. But these are the lessons one learns as President.

Eventually, someone on my staff whispered the suggestion that we ground all air traffic within United States airspace. I concurred, and ordered him to call Dick Cheney and have him take care of that because I was not sure how to do it. All flights were canceled except essential military missions, emergency organ donations, and the Bin-Laden family, who had urgent business in Saudi Arabia to attend to.

Soon thereafter, I was asked to make a statement, which I did. And in that statement I made it clear that I was in charge of the dangerous situation. I was in command of our nation's situations and statements-responding.

We then left the classroom, and I bid farewell to the students and teachers, leaving the matter of the unsatisfactory milk temperature unaddressed. I would deal with that and other concerns when I would pass the No Child Left Behind Act in just a few short years, which stipulated that milk once again be appropriately refrigerated in our schools.

On my way to Air Force One, I learned that yet another plane had struck our homeland. It had been directed directly at our armed forces in the Pentagon. One of the eight sides was struck, and it was destroyed, and there was a tragic loss of life. I had asked Jesus to keep the loss of life at a minimum that day, so my heart went out to those who perished, because the Lord had forsaken them.

The headquarters of our armed defenses was under siege. It was the seat of the most advanced military on Earth, yet they were defenseless against this onslaught of terror.

Since that day, as a result of the tragedy, I have called for our Defense Department to spend some of its large budget on a basic "defense" of our country, and that "strategies" be devised to protect our nation from attack. I have ordered that our military-thinking experts write out such plans so that, in the event that we face the enemy again, we might implement them this time.

But such measures were only distant dreams on September the 11th, 2001.

Soon after the tragic events occurred, it was important that I survey the damaged area from 30,000 feet in the air to get a close look at what we were dealing with. I ordered

Air Force One to fly first to Texas and Louisiana to witness the devastations first hand from that vantage point. Surprisingly, our country looked peaceful in that region. There were white clouds and a lot of blue sky. It was, in fact, quite lovely.

Understandably, everyone's first concern in this day of terror was for the President. If something should happen to the President, America would collapse, and the Constitution would be left vulnerable, having lost its sole protector. Therefore it was decided that I should hide.

Once I was secure, a thousand miles away from danger, I believe that I then thought to ask someone to call my wife and the rest of the White House staff and mention that they might want to run for their lives. If I forgot to do this, let me take this opportunity to apologize to everyone who was in the White House on the morning of September 11th, and assure them that it is a good possibility that they were in my thoughts and prayers at that time.

Air Force One remained in the air for several hours after that. We flew around in circles while the military commanders coordinated our next move. It was a day that tried the nerves of all Americans. And as the Commander in Chief I was not immune from the suffering. In fact, this was one of the most difficult times of the day for me. I was forced to sit through the in-flight movie not once but three times that afternoon.

The movie, I recall very clearly, was *Summer Catch*. I thought it was an excellent movie, combining both romance and baseball, but no one should have to watch it three times in a row. This was yet another in a series of tests of my mettle as President that day.

I would later be taken to a secret military bunker, where I would be advised by the top military minds of my staff.

It was a very expensive and technological bunker, an enormous room filled with screens and monitors. It was like those of the secret-agent movies.

The military experts debriefed me using a very large television-debriefing screen that could switch between maps and pictures and other moving images of terrorists. There may even have been some words on the screen which appeared as though they were being typed out by a computer. Whether they made the impressive "bleeping" sound that letters often make when they appear on a screen in this manner, I do not recall. But it seemed like they should have, so let it reflect in this official record of these events that they did.

In short, I was overwhelmed by the impressive array of stimuli and the flow of complex and secret information. But as I sat and listened to the debriefers, and attempted to concentrate on their presentation, my mind began to wander.

As I beheld these impressive surveillance tools and intelligence-gathering doodads, I remember thinking just one thought: Why couldn't all of these gadgets have been brought to my attention earlier, so that I could have seen how awesome they were as soon as I got to be President?

Since that day, I have not forgotten it, and I have gone back to that secret war room and watched five different baseball games at once on the big screen, with my feet up on the long console with all the fancy buttons, enjoying hot dogs, ice cream, and other delicacies from a fallout shelter storage facility that is rumored to have supplies enough for a thousand years of sporting contests.

I guess that is one small good thing that has come from the horrible happenings of September 11.

After a day of confusion and uncertainty, I addressed the nation from behind the enormous Oval Office desk, and made a mental note to myself that for future Oval Office televisings, I would have this unwieldy desk replaced with one that was several times smaller. This way I would appear much larger, which, in my view, would intimidate and frighten the terrorists, perhaps warding them off, for fear they may face justice at the hands of a President who is over 13 feet tall.

After the speeching, there was no time to rest. Decisions had to be made. Most importantly, who would we blame and subsequently bomb for these horrendous attacks?

No one could have predicted that terrorists would fly planes into the World Trade Center. The only intelligence we had at the time was that terrorists might fly certain cylindrical objects into tall structures of an unknown shape. Only the mystic prognosticators could have put it all together.

I know only one thing: The outlaw who carried out these barbarous acts would be hunted down and smoked out of his hole in the crime-fighting style I employed in Texas. A "Wanted: Dead or Alive" poster would be made to my specifications, and posted throughout Texas and the world. It would be Old West–style justice for the perpetrators of this act. Or failing that, Old West–style justice for those who kind of looked like the perpetrators of this act.

We would keep a keen eye out for such terrorist-looking peoples. The death of Americans would be avenged when the similarly dressed and similarly complected people of Iraq paid dearly for this horrendous act of barbarism. The people of Afghanistan would also pay dearly, as one of the terrorist masterminds had once visited there. They would feel the wrath of the United States for daring to host him in their country. They would be called to account for renting him a room in one of their hotels, or for giving him those small-sized canisters of soap and shampoo in the little basket. They would answer for offering him a towel, and for feeding him a complimentary continental breakfast before he checked out.

In the days that followed, which I believe began on September 12, I felt it was important for me to visit the tiny island nation of Manhattan, to demonstrate how much we, as a nation, cared for its native people. The United States would not stand for this attack against our neighbor. The American people were shaken by this attack on our ally to the North. But though we shared a border with New York, we did not share a common language, and there was no way to express the grief we shared.

While there, I resolved to climb to the top of the pile of rubble left in the wake of the attacks.

It would not be an easy task.

As my feet slipped on the loose stones of the rubble pile, I nearly turned back. But I sensed the people wanted to hear a voice of hope, so I braved onward, not knowing if I would tumble and fall. When I felt the hands of my security detail reach out to aid my ascent, I felt a lump form in my throat. Americans were coming together to help their President in this moment of grave importance to maintain order in his day's schedule.

As I took the bullhorn in hand, I knew that I would

have to call on all of my cheerleading experience to rally the nation through these desperate times. I drew on all the skills I developed cheering the mighty Bulldogs to bring the same game-winning spirit to the tiring rescuers.

I urged the people of the New York race to continue their efforts, which entailed moving the giant pile of rubble elsewhere. We as a nation pledged that day to move that pile to a hole or scrap pile somewhere in New Jersey, I believe.

At the end of the day of September the 11th, as I prepared for bed, I knelt by my bedside and prayed. I counted my blessings. Every such tragic event has a silver lining, and this day was no different. America had a powerful new enemy. An enemy who we could all agree was evil for years to come.

Also, I had faced a trial no President had ever faced, and by the grace of God no President will ever have to face again: I had watched *Summer Catch* three times in one day.

I was consumed with a powerful resolve to exact justice on the offenders of the unspeakable acts which had hit our shores. I would be summoned by the powers of destiny to fulfill the promise I showed as a young child, when I spit grape juice out of my mouth to spray the terrorist beans off of the plate of a nation, and obliterated them by offering them to the dog.

I pledged this to the Almighty that night.

And finally I gave thanks to the Lord that this tragic event would unite the nations of the world behind the trusted foreign-policy leadership of the United States. It would also bring the nations of the United States and New York closer together, allowing Americans of any stripe to enjoy that proud culture's colorful entertain-ments and seasoned flatbreads.

Just before falling asleep, my prayerful emotion gave way to memories of the delicious vanilla-cream cookies that had begun my day, and I thought that it would be a good idea to have a plate of those cookies, and a glass of milk—properly chilled—placed by my bedside from time to time.

16

IT'S A WONDERFUL WAR

No President asks for war. It is always a last re-
sort. Or not a first choice, anyway. Let me put
it this way: It depends on the alphabetical order
of the choices.

And while a President may not ask for war, he may
dream of war. And they are wonderful dreams. They are
dreams in which rose-colored fields of flowered Iraqi grass
sway in the evening breeze. Soldiers prance through green
meadows, smiling, holding hands in the sunshine.

In this glorious dream, the Commander in Chief ap-
pears in the distance like a thousand-story building, he is
a ghostly apparition on the horizon behind the troops, out
of range of the gunfire. He is wearing his flight suit, holding his helmet at his side, urging on our fighting men and

women in their sacred mission with great and inspiring words. Words such as "freedom," "victory," and "bring 'em on."

Soon the soldiers are holding hands with the Iraqi people, who skip happily beside them, gazing with shock, awe, and respect at their liberators. They have received the blessings of freedom, for which they are grateful, and in awe. And shocked.

Beautiful songbirds also chirp in this dream.

Soon the whole world is holding hands and skipping through the happy-fields and enjoying not only the fruits of democracy, but also a bounty of hot dogs — as many as they can eat. Jesus rules benevolently over all the people, looking down lovingly from the heavens. All bask in His unconditional love. Except for terrorists, who are locked away deep in a prison under the world, where no one will ever find them, and where their private parts are electrocuted hourly for all eternity.

Clearly, this is a positive vision for Iraq and the world.

Therefore it came as some surprise to me when I outlined this plan in detail to my military commanders in the spring of 2003, and some of them argued that it was "unrealistic," and "pie in the sky."

"Pie is good," I replied. "Pie is delicious."

My Joint Chiefs of Staff and other advisors explained to me that in order to launch this war, we had to have what in military lingo is known as a "reason."

There were many good reasons to go to war with Iraq. The first one I proposed was that I was the Commander in Chief, and I was ordering it.

When I was told this would not be a good enough reason, more ideas were generated.

One excellent reason, for the moment, was to find Saddam Hussein's weapons of mass destruction, which we had sold to him in the 1980s. I believed strongly that the evil dictator had those weapons, because my Secretary of Defense, Donald Rumsfeld, still had carbon copies of the receipts.

But since the weapons have yet to be found, it is reasonable to assume that the dictator used the art of Iraqi black voodoo to make them disappear.

Another superb reason we thought of was to bring liberty to the people of Iraq. This was a people who above all others on Earth deserved to have the full resources of the United States mobilized to save them from tyranny.

But there was one reason many on my staff believed to be more important than all of the above: Someone had to pay for the attack on our country on September the 11th.

I did not know where the perpetrator, Osama Bin Laden, was hiding at that time. I knew intuitively that he was in a hole, but that was all the information I had. With such vague intelligence, it was not practical for my commanders to formulate a plan to dislodge him from this unknown hole. So, in lieu of him, we settled on someone else: Saddam Hussein.

Let there be no misunderstanding—I did not take any chances selecting someone who may have had nothing to do with a terrorist attack against our country. To be on the safe side, I verified Saddam Hussein's ties to Al-Qaeda with my Jesus-stone. This is a magical amulet that I keep under my desk. I take it out of its velvet sackcloth and hold it aloft only when faced with the most vital decisions facing our country. It seemed to warm in my hands when I passed it over Iraq on my Oval Office map.

White House defense-strategy memo, March 19, 2003

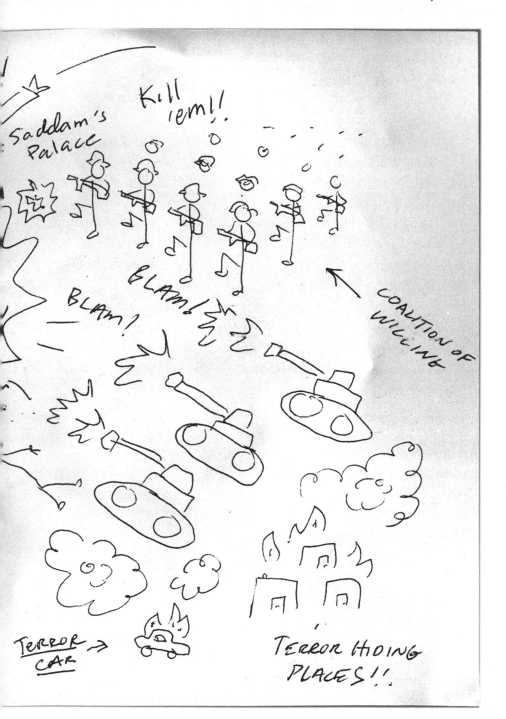

In the face of this compelling evidence, America's mission was clear.

But try as we might, during the first few months of the war, we could not find Saddam Hussein. We put out a reward for his capture. Then we began to get tips that he had fled underground. Into a hole. We then armed our fighting forces with shovels and pickaxes to dig in likely spots across Iraq.

Take back everything I said before about it not being worth finding Osama Bin Laden in a hole. This time, plans were drawn up to dig as many holes as it took to find this substitute culprit of the September 11 attacks.

Eventually, after many months of diligent searching, we succeeded. We found Saddam Hussein in a hole in Iraq. He was not properly groomed, and he smelled of mold.

This is what burrowing does to a man. It makes him like a worm. He loses the ability to see in direct sunlight. He grows little feelers on his lip, which appear to the naked eye to be normal human whiskers. But they are not. They are a mucous membrane not unlike those of the mole, which uses these feelers to sense his way through his labyrinth of tunnels. He burrows down deeper and reproduces with other burrowing vermin. He finds a secluded warren in which to secrete his young, and quickly spawns a race of mutant mole-people.

This is why it was especially important to capture Saddam Hussein in a timely fashion, before he and his army of mole-men could burrow their way to America and attack our homeland from underneath.

The day Saddam Hussein was captured by U.S. forces was one of the greatest moments in the war effort, except perhaps for Mission Accomplished Day. I had promised that the terrorists would be smoked out of their holes, and on that day, this sacred pledge was honored. I cannot say with any certainty whether smoke was used to expel him from that location. But make no mistake: We found him hiding in a dirt hole. And soon he would face justice for being the leader of Iraq.

But let us back up and start the story of the war from its noble beginnings.

Being President is a tremendous honor. There is always somebody there waiting on you. And there is a great deal of free stuff that they give you. They will give you anything you want to eat. A hot dog any time of day! Everything has got the presidential seal on it, too: towels, coasters, the little paper covering on the drinking glasses. Everything. But being President is also an awesome responsibility. And one of those responsibilities is the ability to launch missiles and blow up a whole country.

When it was my turn to blow up a whole country, I took the responsibility very seriously.

In the early morning hours of a particular date in 2003, I believe it was, I gave the order to begin the attack.

In the hours leading up to the attack, much effort was expended in careful consideration and brainstorming by my top military advisors to come up with a name for the war. It is now well known that the name we settled on was "Operation Iraqi Freedom."

But it was not my first choice.

Other choices included "Showdown in the Gulf." At the time it was proposed, we did not know that CNN had already taken it. And there was "Shakedown in the Sand," which I believe the World Wrestling Federation later used when they entertained the troops during their USO tour.

White House memo, October 15, 2002

THE WHITE HOUSE
WASHINGTON

Operation: Squash Terra

nice ring to H ✻ The Terror Zapper

Operation Shocking & Awesome

Target: Some Mideasterners

(Operation: Enduring Terror) *Right feeling*

Righteous Bombing

Operation Blood for Oil

Project Iraqi Pride *Too sensitive*

Too Long Battle for our Very Lives!

(Target Iraqi Butt)

Can I top this one?

Weeks later, after the decision had been made, the name of the war no longer mattered. What mattered was that my staff was assembled, and it was time to start a war. I looked up at them and said solemnly, "It is time to attack Iraq."

As I said it, I realized "Attack Iraq" was the perfect name for this war, because it rhymed. But I had thought of it too late. This was the eleventh hour. All of the government folders with the label "Operation Iraqi Freedom" had already been printed up.

This was to be the first casualty of the war. A reality of wartime that every combatant must face is that there is real loss. The loss of a good name for the war is a setback I did not foresee. But there was no time to mourn. I forged ahead with the bombing campaign.

It was a glorious beginning to freedom in that first 24 hours. Hundreds, perhaps thousands of Iraqi people were killed. And it looked very good on TV, one must admit. It looked just like the 4th of July. Bombs went off, lighting up the night sky with brilliant colors.

If only we could have heard the screams of the dying. Actually, the screams were probably drowned out by the sound of the bombs. That may have been for the best, as the top commanders do not necessarily need to concern themselves with the details.

Our troops behaved bravely in Operation Iraqi Freedom. But of course there are always a few bad apples who violate the rules of war. This happened in the prison "Abu Graheebref."

America does not torture. Therefore, military justice was handed down swiftly against these wrongful torturers. We started at the bottom and worked up the chain of command, all the way to the top. The highest-ranking official involved in the promotion of torture was Private First Class Lynndie England. A court of military justice found that she was solely responsible for the shameful abuse of these prisoners. She was found guilty and is currently serving her prison sentence.

As President, it is my job to say where the "buck stops" in these matters, and I declared decisively in this instance that it stopped with Private First Class Lynndie England.

Some critics point to these bad apples and suggest that they are a reflection of all of our brave fighting men and women. I wish to quickly remind such negative-sayers that my glorious vision for Iraq came from Jesus himself. Are these critics prepared to go on record criticizing the policies of our Lord? I do not think so.

But now is not the time for blaming, blaspheming, or pointing out who failed at what, and which intelligence was false or not. Now is a time to recount the proud history of a President.

One of the most dangerous operations of the war took place late in November, a year or two ago. A plane carrying a very important passenger crept towards Baghdad in the dark of night, protecting this special cargo from terrorists or insurgent attack. The plane landed near the base, and out stepped the President of the United States.

I was quickly ushered into the mess hall, where I served a turkey dinner for the grateful troops, and then bid farewell to the newly liberated and peaceful Iraq, hightailing it out of there to avoid getting killed in the crossfire.

When you bring freedom to a people, sometimes they are so excited to be free that they shoot off rockets and

FROM THE DESK OF
GEORGE. H. W. BUSH

Dear Saddam Hussein,

Please cordially accept my son's invasion of your country.

Sincere personal regards,

George. H. W. Bush

Note from George H. W. Bush to Saddam Hussien,
March 19, 2003

other celebratory explosions to express their great joy of being free.

But perhaps the most historic moment of the Iraq war took place on the deck of the USS *Abraham Lincoln,* which was gleaming in the midday sun on a quiet day in May of 2003.

At a specified moment, an F-18 fighter jet streamed in from the west, blotting out the sun for a split second and causing all eyes on deck to look up in unison. Little did they know that it was a President of a certain United State who was in the passenger seat, being flown there, dressed as though he was the pilot himself.

When they told me I would be flying jets in the National Guard way back in my youth, no one could have guessed the momentous impact it would have. For the culminating moment of my service would happen on this fateful day nearly 30 years later.

It was the most important mission in the war. The final mission. The fighter touched down expertly on the battle-ship's landing strip, and out came a determined leader, to announce to a thankful nation that the war was over and we had been victorious.

The whole world watched in awe that day, as they realized yet again that America had saved the Middle East from chaos.

This was a great moment for our country, and would be the fulfillment of my destiny.

I would like to dedicate this chapter to the brave and resilient people of Iraq, who we had no choice but to attack. They endured our military assault, graciously allowed us to fight the terrorists in their homeland over there so we would not have to fight them over here in ours, and then they rose out of the rubble to take on the challenge of becoming our newest insurgent enemy in the War on Terror.

May God bless them, and bring us swift victory in the fight against them.

17

2004: ANOTHER MANDATE

After I had been in office for a few years, with "Mission Accomplished" under my belt, America's standing in the world at an unprecedented new level, and my successful signing of the Exxon CEO Protection Act, I learned that yet another challenge lay ahead. My advisors informed me that in order to serve the full eight years allotted me by law, I must be "re"-elected.

I began to ponder the purpose of such an undertaking.

What would it serve our country to ask a celebrated War President to jump through this additional hoop? I had been elected once already.

The American people knew that I had stood firm against Evil. They trusted me to put the faith back in science, to keep immigrants from immigranting, and to bring common sense to the debate about whether we should protect the environment. Most importantly, 9-11 had happened on my watch. By any measure, that should count for something.

But as it turns out, my advisors held firm on this "reelection" idea. Therefore, for the second time in four years, I hit the campaign trail.

This time would be different than the last. This time, I had the advantage of what they call "the incumbency": three years of presidenting experience. There was no doubt in my mind that I would win in a landslide. My broader mission to transform our democratatorship was not yet complete, and God knew that.

However, I had not foreseen the lengths to which the Democratic Party, hiding behind the scenes, would go to compete in the race. First, they would put up a candidate to oppose me. Laws had been put in place, I believed, which made such actions illegal. But oppose me they did, even in the face of possible internment at the Guantanamo Bay holding facility.

Next, they would attempt to evade the central issue of this campaign: the raw terror we faced on 9-11.

My staff believed the deep, emotional fear that the terrorists unleashed on September the 11th, the kind of fear that makes a person revert to a primal state in which he cannot use his higher brain functions, was the only issue that the American people were concerned about in this election. They knew the voters were not concerned about "foreign policy," "sound analysis," or "solutions." They simply wanted to be told, again and again, of the terrible, terrifying terror.

Finally, the Democrats boldly attempted to find a candidate who they felt had the best chance of winning.

But they could not find one.

Many opponents emerged from their opponenty enclaves. There was a funny black man. A screaming man. A very old man. And a very small man who appeared to be a troll of some kind. They were all eliminated by infighting, and by the good laws on the books that keep such people out of public office.

After these initial failures, they did not give up their fight. They turned to dark forces, and created a candidate using perverted science. John Kerry was what they called it. It was a monstrosity put together in a madman's secret laboratory, a combination of the living matter of many different candidates. He had the tall, lanky torso of Abe Lincoln, and the brain of my previous opponent, Al Gore. He also had Michael Dukakis's hair, Walter Mondale's charm, and the strong lower jaw of Herman Munster, the great Democratic President of the 1960s.

John Kerry was a scary man, and a scary opponent. His massive block head stared down as he lurched at you, as if reaching for your throat. His face was frozen in a grim scowl, the frightful result of the forbidden experiments of his face-builders. This made him incapable of smiling or showing emotion of any kind, which bespoke the soulless void inside, and its disdain for all humanity.

It was also rumored that some of the body parts used to cobble together this unholy candidate had come from the battlefields of another country from times long past, in the Far East. His expert combiners promoted this fact as if it were a positive attribute. They staged a grand convention in which the monster stood in front of an American flag, and summoned several men who his mad scientist creator had found near-dead on a swift boat. These men proudly took credit for offering an arm or a foot to this abomination so that it might be stitched together against all the laws of God and man.

John Kerry wailed and howled to the domed roof of the convention stadium. His forlorn, walrus-like cries echoed through the expansive hall. The onlookers twisted their faces in a combination of sympathy and disgust, frightened by the cursed freak, yet unable to look away.

When the balloons fell, no one clapped. Instead, all cowered in fear of the monster's wrath.

Many watching the convention on television were swayed by the man-thing's horrid cries. His loud pained sounds stoked a new fear in the voters: the fear that this rampaging monster, once elected, might crush the skulls of their loved ones. This new threat distracted the citizens from the real issue: the raw terror of 9-11. I do not put much stock in polls, but even I was concerned when this so-called "fear gap" began to close.

So I redoubled my campaign efforts. I traveled the country and communicated directly with the American voters.

But this was not as easy as one might think. Not in a world changed forever by the terrible events of 9-11. In speaking to crowds of voters, I faced the real danger that the Enemies of Freedom might infiltrate the audience at one of my stump speeches and attack me with harmful questions.

These enemies had to be stopped.

First, before anyone was admitted into one of my speeches, my staff ran a complete criminal background

THE WHITE HOUSE

WASHINGTON

SPEECH TO NATIONAL FEDERATION OF REPUBLICAN WOMEN

ORLANDO, FL - APRIL 22, 2004

9-11. 9-11. September the 11th, 2001, 9-11. 9-11,
September 11. 9-11 9-11 September 11, 2001, 9-11. 9-11. 9-
11, 9-11, and 9-11.

Cut if passed for time

9-11. 9-11 9-11. September 11, 2001. 9-11. 9-11 9-11, 9-
11 9-11 9-11. September 11th.

September 11, 2001. 9-11. 9-11. ~~September~~ 11, 2001. The
terrible tragedy of September 11. 9-11. 9-11 9-11. 9-11, 9-
11, ~~9-11.~~

9-11 9-11 9-11 September 11, 2001. 9-11. 9-11. 9-11. 9-11
-- 9-11 9-11 9-11 -- 9-11. September ~~the~~ 11th, 9-11. 9-11.
9-11. 9-11, 9-11.

9-11

September 11, 2001. 9-11, 9-11. 9-11. 9-11. 9-11,
9-11 -- 9-11, 9-11, 9-11. 9-11. September 11, 2001.

September the 11th: 9-11. 9-11. 9-11. 9-11. 9-11. Terror
struck. 9-11. 9-11. 9-11. 9-11. September 11. 9-11. 9-11.
9-11-2001. 9-11. September the 11th. September 11th.
September 11th, 9-11. 9-11, September 11. ~~In the wake of~~ 9-
11, 9-11. September 11, 2001. *Emphasize!!*

9-11. 9-11 9-11 9-11 9-11. September 11th, 2001. 9-11,
9-11, 9-11. 9-11, 9-11 September 11th. *(with resolve!)*

Campaign speech transcript with the President's revisions,
April 22, 2004

check and a thorough review of any library books the presumed enemy combatant may have checked out in the last 12 years. Then, using advanced National Security Administration surveillance technology, we analyzed the subject's TV-viewing habits, telephone conversations, and e-mail correspondence. The next step was a DNA check to ascertain U.S.-based parentage, a skin sample for racial analysis, and finally a signed and fingerprinted loyalty oath to ensure lifelong allegiance to the Republican Party and the Bush family.

After all of that, whatever American voter remained— typically on the order of four or five very strong supporters—was permitted to come see their President give a speech.

They were always a very enthusiastic crowd.

Again I began to wonder why it was necessary to go through all the fuss of having an election. Whenever I spoke, Americans overflowed with applause and cheers for my every statement. My staff had amassed stacks of loyalty oaths. Could not these oaths, in some way, be called ballots? I will look into this for future elections, because it would clear away a lot of needless bureaucracy.

The security of our nation is tantamount. And that security must begin with the Commander in Chief. In this first presidential election after the September 11th attacks, Al-Qaeda sympathizers were said to have found sanctuary among the nation's librarians. These terrorists used their wanton access to library books to openly learn about my policies, and conspired to assemble wherever I appeared. They would wave signs and wear T-shirts displaying morally threatening phrases, such as "Peace is an American value" and "Violence is not the answer," which stood in stark contrast to my positive agenda for America.

Fortunately, tough new laws protected me from these evil elements of our homeland. My staff was able to create "free-speech cages" that would allow the banner wavers and T-shirt wearers to shout and speak as freely as they wished, far away from where they could be heard. There they could then proudly exercise their first-amendment rights, just like the great baboons in our nation's zoos.

Criticism of the Commander in Chief is the greatest security threat we face in the 21st century. This is one of the vital lessons we learned after 9-11. Such open questions brought comfort to our enemies abroad, who hate us and want to destroy our democratic values. When they see us living according to those values, it brings them comfort. And we must not comfort them. We must agitate them like one agitates a hornets' nest. You must whack the hive with a stick. Bash it and keep bashing it. But whatever you do, do not let the hornets see you exercising your freedom. Then they will really come after you.

Even though I brought my winning strategy, and the date of September the 11th, before the American electorate time and time again, I faced a continuing threat of the John Kerry monster. As he campaigned, lumbering about with his arms outstretched, an alarming number of Americans began to embrace this creation of the dark sciences. And it soon became clear that I would have to meet the creature head on, in open debate.

There are legitimate questions to be raised regarding whether it is appropriate in a time of war for another member of the government to debate a sitting President. The American people must present a united front in war.

Otherwise, our enemies might see that we have open debate and free discussion. The troops on the battlefield must know that they are fighting for something much greater than that.

The debates were much ballyhooed. I did not realize it at the time, but I did fairly well. I would express my cogent remarks to the people, and in response the Kerry-thing would yell and groan in unintelligible, unnatural moans. I could only hope that the monstrosity's message did not resonate with voters.

I prayed for a mob of townspeople to hunt him down with torches and burn him in the public square, as they had done with the monsters of lore. But our civilization has grown too tolerant of the half-living.

To be on the safe side, I had a secret weapon in the debate. With this weapon, I would be able to respond forthrightly and directly, without all of the cumbersome memorizing required as in the debates of the past. The latest developments in electronic earpiece technology had finally caught up to the needs of the modern President. An earpiece connected to a receiver, hidden discreetly under my suit jacket, allowed my staff to alert me to any national-security emergencies that might take place during the debate.

When one is President, one must always be ready to respond to issues of the highest national significance at a moment's notice. During a debate, my advisors might have to suddenly call out to me, "Mister President, stop smirking." Or "Sir, quit pursing your lips," and other threats to the nation, which I had a sacred responsibility to address immediately and decisively.

My opponent was just such a threat. If he were to turn and lunge at me unpredictably, I needed a warning from my secret service detail. That warning would be delivered through the earpiece, just in time for me to evade his attack, and perhaps light him on fire with my wooden torch, which I kept under my podium for just such an emergency. If called upon to do so, I would thrust it at the monster to keep him at bay, for he did not understand fire.

Early in the campaign, I developed a comprehensive fire-based strategy to defeat my easily frightened opponent. This tactic was used to great effect in my eventual victory. Every day on the campaign trail I would put forth a message involving fire. "Fire, good!" I would say. My opponent was forced to respond by bellowing the slurred words, "Fire, bad!" and blocking his eyes from the threat of fire. Sometimes he would smash through the nearest wall in a vain hope to escape from an imagined fire.

As Election Day grew near, I focused on the important issues: 9-11, September the 11th, and the events of 9-11, 2001. On the road, I would practice repeating my important stances on these issues: "9-11, 9-11, 9-11," I would say over and over again until I could do so without thinking.

This clear message had to be communicated to the American people if I was to be elected again. And I did so. A great deal. People became hypnotized by my wise words. My 9-11 9-11 9-11 proposal, which was presently being debated in the Congress, as well as my urgent call to 9-11 9-11 September 11th and 9-11 were making good sense to voters.

Finally the day of reckoning came, and to my dismay, the exit polls indicated that the monster was getting more votes than I was.

I was concerned. I prayed to Jesus, asking "Why have you forsaken me, Lord?" I cursed him and all his so-called "holy" powers. What good was he if he could not deliver this vital election? I renounced the Holy Father and cast my lot with the stone idols of Babylon. Perhaps they would be more responsive to my fevered prayers.

Then my experts advised me that votes cast early in the day tend to be more sympathetic to re-animated, half-dead candidates. This brought me no comfort. What if my message had not reached enough voters? What if I had alienated the anti-fire vote? And what of the sheer terror of 9-11? My mind was racing, and I began to feel dizzy, filled with curses and uncertainty.

But my momentary spell of doubt was unfounded.

When the votes had all been counted, I was declared the winner. The people had given me a clear mandate with one of the widest margins of the popular vote in a U.S. presidential election in this century. I won both the popular and the Electoral College vote. I apologized to Jesus for doubting Him, accepted Him back into my heart, and bid my substitute Babylonian deities good day.

The exit polls proved more wrong than they ever had before. The trend on that day was clearly for George W. Bush. Even some of the new electronic voting machines were catching on to the excitement and casting votes for me, correcting the errant judgment of the voters.

This great victory provided me with a mandate to carry out my campaign promises of 9-11, terror, and 9-11 to the fullest extent possible.

As for my one-time opponent, legend has it that even now he continues to lurk in Washington, awaiting his chance for a second grotesque run for the presidency.

But it is unlikely that he will succeed. I do not believe that any voting bloc will ever endorse a Frankenstein's

THE WHITE HOUSE
WASHINGTON

August 29, 2005

Dear Oscar Mayer Hot Dog Company,

I am writing this letter to express my great satisfaction with your new wiener product, OSCAR MAYER® BUN-LENGTH®, which truly offers hot dog in every bite of the bun. I did not know such a hot dog was available on the market until I asked the White House chef why the bun and the wiener always seemed to be unaligned. It was then that he procured your product.

Besides its improved length, the taste of the wiener is also commendable. It was at once succulent, delicious, easy to eat, and satisfying. I enjoyed my meal with ketchup, mustard, and a bit of relish. That is the way I like a hot dog to be served.

As President, every day I am faced with any number of stressful decisions and demands, and having access to bun-length wieners takes a significant amount of that stress away. Words cannot describe the great joy you have brought to my heart.

Keep up the good work, and God bless you.

With deepest admiration,

George W. Bush

GWB: pjc

Letter to Oscar Mayer, August 29, 2005

monster for the nation's highest office, unless those voters are elderly blind men or naive little girls of a gentle demeanor. But even those voters, in the end, will be destroyed by the monster, for he cannot control his urges. His untamed emotions and great strength will crush the people he is charged to protect.

He is not meant to live among us.

But as to me, the mandate holder, how will history view my legacy? Will I be celebrated with parades and flowers tossed at my feet when I retire? Or will I enjoy the noble yet quiet honor of having a rocket ship named after me? Only time and subsequent chapters of this book will tell.

18

MY ENDURING LEGACY:
MOUNT RUSHMORE?

How a nation should honor a President who has made great sacrifices to serve is a difficult question. But it is an important one, and one which we must consider fully and thoughtfully.

As such matters are discussed, it is vital to remember that concerns about a legacy can never be a factor in the day-to-day decisions that a President makes. All a President's decisions affect the country—and history—and therefore cannot be taken lightly. But when history is written, everyone who is alive today will be dead, and therefore history does not matter. Nor can a President base his decisions on the so-called "learning" of the past. The past is gone, and is best forgotten.

The people who may be alive in future times will live by these same constraints. They will be unable to learn from our example. We wish them good luck.

All a President can do is make decisions based on the facts of the present which he chooses to accept. That means he must rely on the only tools he has available to him: his gut instincts, and the Word of God, which together are never wrong, as long as the latter is properly interpreted from scripture, and the former is not adversely effected by acidic foods.

In this written work, I offer my counsel on the pivotal matter of how my legacy must be honored. There are any number of statues, memorials, or symbolic public monuments that would be appropriate to honor the first two-term President of a new century: from the grand visages hewn in the very rock on Mt. Rushmore, to the small but stately minting of a likeness on the nation's coins.

Of these proposed solutions, I strongly believe that a large statue is called for, and I propose that this towering likeness be built in the glorious city center of the new, re-built New Orleans. I propose that this structure be made of rock-hard stone, a stone which will never fade or wither with time. I do not know what the types of stone are, but a strong stone is called for. Whether that be marble, or granite, or just regular rock, I leave for the stone carvologists to determine.

As for what the likeness should entail, perhaps the moment to be captured in stone is when I stood upon the USS *Abraham Lincoln* and proclaimed that the Iraq war was won. Alternately, the moment I stood atop the ruins of the Twin Towers on or about September the 11th, 2001, after that city was attacked.

The statue should be 900 feet tall, and be a gleaming remembrance for all the people of New Orleans to enjoy. A celebration of the President who fought to protect them from evil, and who personally flew in to hug some people on TV in the wake of the great Hurricane Karmina.

A grand painting must also be done, as is the tradition in our great country. This portrait will hang in the hallowed halls of the White House for as long as the United States lasts. As the artist reflects on this large framed work, he will surely wonder how history will paint my legacy. Will there be the bright yellows of hope? The blood red of slain terrorists, who faced justice? Or the soothing purples of royalty? Or will it be a mural of blazing colors, exploding with triumph of a resolute and determined President?

Someone worthy, who knows coloring, must take up the painter's trowel and start creating this art. But who is more familiar with me than me? Since I know what should be said about me, and by contrast, what should be left to the inferrers, I recommend that the commissioned artist turn to the words in this book for inspiration. By reading my thoughts in these pages, the art-maker might capture the essence of my legacy directly from the mouth of the horse, so to speak.

One of the traditions of the nation's chief executive is that once he has left the office he is expected to found a presidential library, in which all of his presidential letters, memoranda and papers are archived for the people and the scholars and the triviologists to examine.

I have begun exploring my options in this regard. Firstly, I have decided that all of my papers will be sealed in an underground vault for 2,000 years so that no one will

THE WHITE HOUSE
WASHINGTON

Books for the Bush Presidential Library

The Bible

The Bible Study Guide

Encyclopedia of Baseball

~~TV Guide~~ (Too hard to keep current)

Memo, April 17, 2006

ever be able to see them. Perhaps the locked and guarded steel entrance to this vault could be housed within my presidential library.

I wish to employ 21st-century technology in my presidential library. It is time, I believe, to no longer look at the past, but to the future. A George W. Bush Presidential Library and Detention Facility will reflect the permanent changes in the world that took place after September 11, 2001. In this world, all of the patrons that enter my library must be thoroughly searched, screened for weapons, undergo a criminal background check, and have their medical records reviewed for any sign of disease.

Lastly, my library itself will be a memorial to the victims of the great tragedy of 9-11. It will be shaped as a memorial to the Twin Towers after September the 11th: a giant pile of rubble. There will not be any books inside of the library. All of the books will be in a pile atop the rubble, burned beyond readability. For a fitting tribute, I propose one burned book for every victim of that great tragedy. Those who wish to attempt to read one of these books will have to dig it out of the rubble and ash, as a way to honor the sacrifice of the heroic workers who cleared the pile of rubble after the hallowed attacks.

One important note: The books should be piled up and burned in accordance with the Dewey Decimal System.

Many have asked me what I will do once I have retired from the presidency. First, I have not made up my determination one way or the other whether I will retire or not. It is possible that Congress will pass a law allowing a President to rule for more terms in office, like in the days of history. We all know from our text books that the great FDR ruled for three or perhaps four terms as President. And do not forget George Washington, the storied father of our country, who sat on the throne for 200 years.

It is also possible that a terrible tragedy will befall our nation, and I will have no choice but to declare a national state of emergency and suspend the Constitution in order to protect our cherished liberties. In this eventuality, the electoral process would be discontinued indefinitely. I hope this does not happen, but one never knows when such extreme measures are necessary to protect us against the enemy.

I have vowed to stay the course, and that could mean a quarter-century or more in the White House. We still have many goals to achieve, and if we are to keep that sacred trust, my vision for the country must be followed through to its completion, as foretold in the Book of Revelations. That is, at least until the appearance of the seven-headed beast and the descent of all non-believers into the pit of fire.

Perhaps, at that time, I will accept a position at the right hand of Christ. I should point out that no official offer has been made, as of this writing, regarding my role in the next life, or my particular position during the Rapture proceedings. Therefore I will not speculate further on that. Let me just put it this way: I am hopeful that Jesus has been impressed by my good work, and that there will be high-level talks to determine my rightful place.

But should circumstances force me to abdicate this office, whether it be in 30 or even 40 years, I shall have to ask myself the difficult question: Where can one go after being President of the United States? What can one do to top the experience of fighting for our very freedoms, of holding each and every American citizen's life in one's protective embrace?

The answer is clear. Major League Baseball Commissioner. Nothing would make me prouder, or cap off my illustrious career in the private sector or in public service better than that proud distinction.

I would have a big office with pennants hanging in it. I would go to games, and congregate with the players, and wave to crowds from the stands from the Commissioner's honored box seat. I would get to wear a baseball cap, almost to no end. And Jesus would be by my side, eating a hot dog, and smiling for my good fortune.

I pledge that I would fulfill the duties of Baseball Commissioner honorably.

I endeavor always to place my vision for the future within the realm of what is realistic, so perhaps it is inappropriate for me to touch on the subject that follows. But I feel that if this manuscript is to be the definitive record of my life and works, all matters must be addressed. I speak of the prospect that my name will inspire the creation of a new candy bar.

If my legacy is to inspire the creation of a sugared snack food, let my discourse within these pages be considered my last will and testament in that regard.

I do not wish coconut to be included. Coconut has a stringy texture, and I do not like it. This holds for whether the candy be in the form of a bar, a chew, a cup, a cake, or a ball. However, one or more of the following ingredients will be acceptable in combination: peanuts, almonds, nougat, milk chocolate, or caramel. And perhaps a "crunch" item, whether that be a toffee, cookie, or crisp-based material yet to be devised by candy science.

Dark chocolate, while in favor with some, will not be permitted on or in the bar. This shall be the case in any form the candy may take, even if packaged in a box as kernels, pieces, minis, nuggets, or bits. A truly American snack-treat must be covered in milk chocolate only. Dark chocolate may be suitable for a snack created to honor the dignitary of another country, but not the United States of America.

A treat devised within these specifications would be a suitably honorific honor to bestow upon a President.

My genetic legacy is not as easy to determine.

While it is evident that the Bush name will not live on through my children, since my daughters' eventual offspring will bear the names of their hapless husbands, the Bush family will nonetheless live on.

Perhaps when history needs it most, my cherished bloodline will reappear in someone named George Walker Peterson or George Walker Jones, and this progeny of mine will lead the country in a time of great crisis. A time, perhaps, when even bolder executive authority is called for in a future age that may bring terrors even more terrifying than the terrorists.

The mind sputters at the notion.

But at this time, I must put all of my faith in my brother Neil's mentally challenged son, Pierce. It is up to him to seed the Bush future. And perhaps he will be our country's first retarded President, a shining example to other retarded presidential hopefuls across our great land. And while being retarded may be a handicap in the office of President, I have faith that his Bush instincts will raise him above his mental disabilities. We must not be prejudicial in this matter, for the Constitution does not expressly forbid a Retard–American from occupying the highest office in the land.

A dominant Bush family trait is that of Christian charity. It is in my nature to be giving to those I choose, and my post-elective years will be no different.

Like all ex-Presidents, especially the noted Jimmy Carter, who has so inspired the world with his good works in retirement, I too will find a particular calling that I will make my signature issue. I will establish a foundation to focus on this issue.

My signature issue, I have decided, will be golf.

I will work hard to ensure that golf is enjoyed in all corners of the civilized world by my colleagues and me. I will appeal to the better nature of my fellow citizens to donate their dollars to this worthy cause, so that I might play with only the most enjoyable golfers, and the newest and highest-quality golf clubs, and never have to worry about where my next tee or ball is coming from.

Surely, we can all agree that this is a positive vision for making the world a better place. Like President Carter before me, I will build a humanitarian organization around my important cause. I will call it "Habitat for Golf." Under the noble charter of this foundation, volunteers, church groups, and others will build golf courses all around the world, so that I might always have a place to golf, no matter where my vacation travels might take me.

One very important thing I am looking forward to in my retirement is spending more time on my ranch in Crawford, Texas, with my brush. It seems that no matter how much of it I clear, it is never fully cleared. I clear some on my vacation, I go back to work, but when I come back again, it is all regrown. It is very frustrating.

Finally, I will have the time necessary to clear it all, and clear it for good. I want to do this so that my family and I can enjoy a life on the flat Texas plains, unencumbered by plants or foliage of any kind.

In looking back at all I have accomplished in my time in office, I cannot help but feel a deep sense of pride in not only my achievements, but in the shared achievement-making of the brave men and women who served with me.

We all worked together to make America a better place. We leave the world a little less terrorized than how we found it. We led the country in war, we worked to protect marriage from the wrongful marriers, and we fought to save Social Security and Medicare from the nation's seniors.

If the next great leader of our nation should desire it, and has the foresight to ask, I will give him much-needed advice. And that goes for any world leaders of other countries, as well. I fully expect that the job of governing in the 21st century will not get easier. It will only get more complicateder.

For any concern of governance that you may have, I will continue, whether through my own acts or through those of my progeny, to be bound by a sacred trust to offer my wisdom of statecraft.

I shall forever be committed to serve, pledged to lead, and destined for destiny.

PHOTO CREDITS

Back flap: Permission for use and alteration granted by Getty Images. Pages 45, 51, and 55: Permission for use granted by George Bush Presidential Library. Page 69: Permission for use and alteration granted by George Bush Presidential Library. Page 91: REUTERS/Gerald Schuman. Page 105: AP/WIDE WORLD PHOTOS. PHOTO INSERT: photos 1, 2, 3, 4, 5, 6, 7, 8, 10, 12, 13—permission for use and alteration granted by George Bush Presidential Library; photos 9, 11, 14, 16, 18, 20, 22, 24—permission for use and alteration granted by AP/WIDE WORLD PHOTOS; photos 19, 21, 23—permission for use and alteration granted by Getty Images; photo 15—U.S. Air Force photo released as public domain; photo 17—U.S. Navy photo released as public domain.